Self and Spirit in the Therapeutic Relationship

D0161934

Centred on an understanding of the self, *Self and Spirit in the Therapeutic Relationship* acknowledges the spiritual component in therapy and healing, but places it firmly within a psychological framework. Kenneth Bragan has written an engaging account of his journey towards understanding the psyche, drawing on a wide range of reading and personal experience. He shares with the reader how Kohut's theories about the self have illuminated his own clinical work and explains simply what these ideas are.

Beginning with a brief account of the early development of self, the author moves on to discuss the different functional aspects of the self. He focuses on the crucially important concept of 'selfobject' and uses examples from a variety of literary texts to demonstrate mirroring, idealizing, growth and disorders.

Kenneth Bragan's unique approach will provide those training to be psychotherapists and counsellors with a thought-provoking and accessible introduction to ideas about the self. In addition *Self and Spirit in the Therapeutic Relationship* addresses a question which is becoming increasingly urgent for many people: must we simply resign ourselves to the spiritual poverty of these times?

Kenneth Bragan was Senior Psychiatrist at Ashburn Hall Hospital, Dunedin, New Zealand before his retirement and was a Fellow of the Australian and New Zealand College of Psychiatrists.

Self and Spirit in the Therapeutic Relationship

Kenneth Bragan

London and New York

First published 1996
by Routledge
11 New Fetter Lane, London EC4P 4EE

Simultaneously published in the USA and Canada
by Routledge
29 West 35th Street, New York, NY 10001

© 1996 Kenneth Bragan

Typeset in Times by LaserScript, Mitcham, Surrey
Printed and bound in Great Britain by
TJ Press (Padstow) Ltd, Padstow, Cornwall

British Library Cataloguing in Publication Data
A catalogue record for this book is available from the British Library

Library of Congress Cataloguing in Publication Data
A catalogue record for this book has been requested

ISBN 0–415–12787–4 (hbk)
ISBN 0–415–12788–2 (pbk)

To bring up, out of the web of
world happening, a millennium of
organic culture-history as an
entity and a person, and to grasp
the conditions of its inmost
spirituality – such is the aim.

Spengler

The salvation of souls seems too speculative a job. I think if a man is
truly a man, true to his own being, his soul saves itself in that way. But
no two people can save their souls alive in the same way. As far as
possible, we must leave them to it.

D.H. Lawrence

Contents

	Acknowledgements	ix
	Prologue	1
1	The self in being	15
2	The self in action	26
3	The self in becoming	36
4	The self in disorder	48
5	The self in recovery	58
6	The bridge	69
7	The spirit in essence	81
8	The spirit in action	93
	Epilogue	106
	Bibliography	116
	Index	118

Acknowledgements

The author and publisher would like to thank the copyright holders for granting permission to reprint extracts from the following:

The Inner Reaches of Outer Space by Joseph Campbell, copyright © 1986: reproduced by permission of Harper & Row, Publishers, Inc.;

The Poetic Image by C. Day Lewis, copyright © 1961: reproduced by permission of Thames & Hudson Ltd;

Trauma and Recovery by Judith Lewis Herman, copyright © 1992; reproduced by permission of Basic Books, a division of HarperCollins Publishers Inc.;

The Politics of Experience and the Bird of Paradise, copyright © R.D. Laing, 1967: reproduced by permission of Penguin Books Ltd;

The Metaphor of Play by Russell Meares: reproduced by permission of the author;

Interview with Carl Rogers in *The Use of Self in Therapy*, edited by M. Baldwin and V. Satir, copyright © 1987, pages 47 and 50: reproduced by permission of The Haworth Press, Inc., New York;

Real Presences by George Steiner: reproduced by permission of Faber & Faber Ltd;

The Interpersonal World of the Infant by Daniel N. Stern, copyright © 1987: reproduced by permission of Basic Books, a division of HarperCollins Publishers Inc.

Every effort was made to clear permission of all extracts reprinted in this book, and the publisher would be very happy to hear from copyright holders whom we are unable to trace.

Prologue

This book centres on the clinical relevance of the self, and is the culmination of a journey that began twenty years ago when I was first introduced to that subject by Heinz Kohut's *The Analysis of the Self*. From that book I got the impression that here was an approach that was not only new, but also promised a clearer understanding of the psyche and the healing potential of psychotherapy. Kohut's second book confirmed this. It was more confident and clear in establishing a view distinctly different from classical psychoanalysis and, with its resounding title, *The Restoration of the Self*, seemed to promise to bring new life into psychotherapy. Since then Self Psychology has become established as a powerful force within psychoanalysis, and perhaps even more so in psychotherapy in general: the importance of an understanding of the self in therapy is now firmly established. That the recognition of the clinical relevance of the self has been occurring at this particular time deserves a little attention, as it has some bearing on understanding both the significance and the course of the developments.

The terrible wars and great social turmoil of this century, as well as the rapidity of change and increasing pace of life, along with decline in religious beliefs, have all been having a shattering effect on the cultural foundations of the sense of individuality which we call the self, an effect which has been graphically described by one who suffered more than most from these happenings.

In his autobiographical *The World of Yesteryear* Stefan Zweig writes of his early years in Vienna at the beginning of this century: 'One was not a Viennese without this love for culture, without this sense, aesthetic and critical at once, of the holiest exuberances of life.' The peace and culture of those early years generated an exuberance for life, a passionate engagement which stayed with Zweig throughout the terrible years of loss and deprivation that followed. During those years, fleeing first from Austria and then from France, he lost home and country, as well as a good deal of his literary work. Yet he was able to retain a determined dedication to his craft as a writer, as well as to an unshakeable humanism. This is how he describes the depredations of those years:

> We, who have been hounded through all the rapids of life, we who have been torn loose from all the roots that held us, we, always beginning anew when we have been driven to the end, we, victims and yet willing servants of unknown, mystic forces, we, for whom comfort has become a saga and security a childhood dream, we have felt the tension from pole to pole and the eternal dread of the eternal now in every fibre of our being.

This, on the grand scale, is the story of this century and, although Zweig's experience may have been extreme, those of us who have not been aware of such turmoil and insecurity may not have been allowing ourselves a full recognition of the reality of the times, and the way things have changed. Zweig also comments on the increase in busy-ness and clamour of life, and the effects this has on the self:

> But is not ours a time which does not grant, even to the purest and most secluded, any quiet for waiting and ripening and contemplating and collecting oneself, as it was granted to the men of the better and calmer pre-war period.

So the emergence of recognition of the clinical relevance of the self has been happening at a time when the full impact of the shaking of the cultural foundations of the self has been having its effect. It has also been happening when the cult of individualism has been reaching a peak, when the importance of the individual has more than ever been emphasized.

The strain generated by this could not have been other than great. Possibly because of this, and the pressing urgency of keeping the self grounded and cohesive in the face of life's increasing complexity, the interest in the self has been pushed in the direction of the clinical, rather than the wider aspects of understanding of the self to be found in literature and general knowledge. Yet such is the present state of turmoil and fragmentation that a more general understanding would seem to be urgently needed, and in the hope of reaching towards this we will start with the clinical but then extend into literature and into the spiritual domain. When we do this, we find that not only have poets and writers generally demonstrated and expressed a cultural and spiritual awareness of the self, they have also anticipated many of the findings of Self

Psychology. Kohut referred to this as the anticipatory function of art, and it is something that will contribute a lot to this text.

Kohut's development of a different theoretical perspective stemmed from work with people with narcissistic personality disorders, particularly from the experience of the patient coming to depend absolutely on the on-going presence of the therapist, and on the therapist being available in particular ways: some needing the therapist simply to reflect them (which he termed the mirror transference) and some needing the therapist to be a god-like figure (the idealizing transference). The reality of this dependence became evident whenever the analyst failed to meet the particular needs of the patient, by not responding in the way required or by having to miss regular contact for any reason. Analysts' holidays presented a particular problem, and commonly there would be a flare-up of symptoms or breakdown of behaviour at such times.

Experiences like these led him to recognize that, in addition to symptoms or problems caused by internal conflict, there could also be deficiencies of the self resulting from lack of needed nurturance and responsiveness during the developmental years. When such deficits are present, they can be re-awakened in the relationship with the analyst and then have a determining effect on the transference. The weakened area of the self is strengthened through the bond with the analyst, but at first a guarantee of the therapist's presence is necessary to maintain this. When this fails, for any reason, the self collapses in strength or fragments.

On the basis of experiences of this sort, Kohut claimed that, to comprehend the psyche in its full complexity, a 'self' psychology was necessary in addition to the 'drive' psychology of classical psychoanalysis. Furthermore, he suggested that the tool for gathering the data essential to understanding complex mental states is empathy, the vicarious introspection of seeing into oneself in order to see into another. He referred to this as an 'experience-near' approach, in contrast to the 'experience-distant' approach of objective science. He nevertheless claimed that it was equally scientific.

At the same time as I was being introduced to Kohut's ideas I happened to become interested in the life and work of D.H. Lawrence, and was immediately struck by a strong similarity between his views and those of Kohut. In *Fantasia of the Unconscious*, for instance, Lawrence writes:

> Let me say that to my mind there is a great field of science which is as yet quite closed to us. I refer to the science that proceeds in terms of life and is established on the data of living experience and of sure intuition. Call it subjective science if you like.

This is surely the same notion as the 'experience-near' scientific approach of Kohut, and what is so important about it is the acknowledgement it gives to the role of inner experience and the importance of empathy. We are what we are because, not only do we interact, we experience the interaction, and much of what we become is determined by that experience. For Lawrence, any psychology that does not give acknowledgement to that inevitably dehumanizes, which is what he would have seen behaviourism doing.

Lawrence also made the same distinction between the core self and the ego as is made by Kohut. He referred to the former as 'I-am-I in vital centrality' and to the latter as 'I-am-I in distinction from a whole universe which is not I' – in other words, one is the engaged self of pure subjectivity and the other the self of self-awareness. The former, the core self, is particularly susceptible to the vicissitudes of empathy, while the latter, the ego, is primarily concerned with attachment and the discharge of drive.

For me, this was not only an exciting discovery but it started a process which has continued uninterruptedly over the years since: a process of concurrent exploration in both literature and the developments occurring in psychotherapy. It was a process that seemed to gather its own momentum and not only did it provide interesting cross-fertilization and at times confirmation, but gradually the two streams merged and carried me into the province of spirituality.

Another feature of this process has been the uncanny way in which one thing led to another: how the right book seemed to appear at the right time; the way in which having started on the journey the next step just seemed to emerge. While appreciating this, and being wryly amused by it at times, I attempted to make little of it. Although I was also reading a good deal of C.G. Jung, I preferred to remain agnostic regarding synchronicity and such apparently mystical notions. Nevertheless the experience was real and, even though Jung's formulations have little place in this book, I feel he has been an important presence.

In one particular respect, however, Jung's theory must be mentioned, and that is the importance of his concept of individuation, because, as well as giving central significance to the developing self, this concept also gives it a source and a destination. Jung's concept of individuation as a process prompted from within by the archetypal Self gives the self a clear biological grounding, which is lacking in the psychoanalytic view. In his book *Archetype: A Natural History of the Self* Dr Anthony Stevens has marshalled convincing evidence, biological and ethological, to support Jung's concept of archetypes and the collective unconscious, and this view adds another dimension to what is going to be an important theme for us: the process and the fundamental importance of reciprocity. Stevens quotes Kepler's dictum: 'For to know is to compare that which is externally perceived with inner ideas and to judge that it agrees with them.' In other words, it is when inner programming fits with objective reality that true knowledge is acquired. Konrad Lorenz takes this away from an idealist position by pointing out that the very means of perception and registering of the external world are part of that reality. He writes: 'The physiological mechanism whose function it is to understand the real world is no less real than the world itself.' So, it is when innate dispositions fit reciprocally with the objective reality they meet that knowledge is acquired; and it is when the innate disposition towards actualization of the archetypal Self meets a reciprocating presence that the self is born and grows (and if that is true, what an important truth it is to know). Archetypes are biologically grounded internal dispositions, which at first have no psychic content, and the archetypal Self is the inner prompt to selfness. In this way Jung provides a biological grounding for the self, and in doing so gives Self Psychology a firmer base.

Another important aspect of Kohut's theory of the self is that the self has two poles. At one pole is the infant's need to be affirmed and encouraged in its authentic being and its own achievements (the mirroring pole) and at the other is the infant's need to gain strength from feeling part of, or being identified with, someone or something experienced as strong and reliable (the idealizing pole). The former need is met by mirroring from the care-taking person. Prototypically this is the gleam in mother's eye as she sees her child's essential being emerge. Good mirroring not only affirms, it also guides the child in discovering what is possible and safe. It helps children find their true potential and therefore it requires that the essential self of the child is truly seen. Once established, such a process leads the child to a sense of enjoyment of his or her own capabilities, fuels self-esteem and a sense of worth, and forms a basis for developing ambition and a sense of self-pride. Developmental deficits in the mirroring pole result in a dependence on others for a sense of self-esteem and self-worth, a hunger for affirmation and a persisting need for support.

Idealization is the process by which the child at first is comforted and reassured by being held in mother's arms, and later finds strength by identifying with an idealized other or with idealized values and aims. This pole of the self gives life direction and structure, knowledge of right and wrong, and a sense of self-control. Deficits result in feelings of weakness, aimlessness and not being in charge of one's life.

These, in brief outline, are the two poles of the self: fundamental concepts of Self Psychology which add greatly in practice to the understanding of transference. In addition, however, Kohut postulated that between the two poles there is a tension arc made up of the natural skills and talents of the child, and that the development of these is promoted by what he termed 'alter ego' or 'twinship' experiences, by which he means the sense of being alongside and in intimate contact with a self of similar nature and potentialities. When this self-other state is established, as for instance in a close peer relationship, the child learns new skills by imitation of others, be they parents or siblings or peers, and also grows in self-confidence.

Each of these processes – mirroring, idealizing and alter ego – promote the growth of the self, and those objects, be they people or things, that function in such a way that they provide that sort of experience, are called selfobjects. This word 'selfobject' is confusing, and part of the confusion comes from its including the word 'object', although it designates something that is subjective.

The concept of selfobject is to be given a place of central importance here, along with reciprocity, because they are seen as the significant bridges which reach out from psyche to spirit. For those not *au fait* with the concept of selfobject a full understanding will come only as the text proceeds, but a brief introduction may help.

Any person or object experienced as having a self-discovering, self-promoting or self-strengthening function is a selfobject. However, it is the *experience* of the object that matters, not the external reality, not the actuality, and selfobjects must be clearly distinguished not only from the external objects that are the focus of the experience but also from internal representations of objects and from self-representations. The concept is difficult to grasp because it is purely subjective. Its reality is in the inner world, and it is best to think of it simply as how an object is experienced. Selfobjects are the self-fortifying internal reflection of the outer world, the internal soil in which a cohesive self can grow.

And this is an appropriate place to emphasize that what is being offered here is not a comprehensive approach to psychopathology or to therapy, but rather an approach that is solely involved with the self and does not include other crucially important parts of the inner world that are 'not-self'. Internal representations of objects, which are so important in understanding particular mental states, and are emphasized by the object relations school of psychoanalysis, are part of the 'not-self'. So are the archetypes of the 'objective psyche' of the Jungian school. These inner configurations are not part of the self and therefore do not function as selfobjects, although perhaps it could be said that when a living connection is established with an archetype then it does become a selfobject. So what is being offered here is partial and limited, and it in no way encroaches upon, or detracts from, the major systems of under-standing psychopathology and the processes of therapy. Its only focus is the centred self.

By their presence, selfobjects create the self's inner space and promote its strength, and, as experiences of mirroring, idealizing and alter ego presence do that, so the child becomes decreasingly dependent on the immediate presence of the objects that provide the function. Presence in fantasy becomes sufficient for increasing periods of time, so that, when selfobject experience is adequate, dependence on the imme-diate presence of the providers gets less and less, although complete independence does not occur. Frequent recharges and a continuing background of supply are required if fragmentation of the self is not to be a threat.

Self Psychology does not see the aim of psychological development to be independence, for dependence on selfobject experience remains throughout life. Rather, the aim is the development of an inner strength that frees from addictive patterns of need and attachment, from 'childish' dependence.

Where there has been significant selfobject failure, particularly in the earliest years, the self remains fragile and prone to fragmentation, and when fragmentation occurs more intense selfobject needs emerge. These so-called 'archaic' selfobject needs are the self's need for absolute certainty of the selfobject presence at the earliest stages of development, as well as the need to be able to control the object. When they emerge as a result of later collapse, and this often happens in therapy, such intense selfobject needs have the same characteristics, of requiring total reliability and security of possession, that characterize early childhood. These are the needs underlying some of the 'transferences' that commonly occur in therapy, and this will be enlarged upon later.

The concept of the bi-polar self is centrally important to Self Psycho-logy, as well as being distinctive to it, and is going to be another important strand in this text. The concept received strong confirmation of its value in the understanding of human development and personality functioning when two major biographies were published – the recent biographies of George Bernard Shaw and Oscar Wilde. This con-firmation came in their providing almost pure examples of the two poles of the self, as described by Kohut.

Shaw and Wilde were great playwrights, but they were also great individualists who came to prominence in London society when individualism as an ideal was first coming into vogue. They arrived in England within a year of each other, both with the avowed intention of becoming famous and both having sufficient genius to support their grand aspirations: the one as a flickering flame, the other as an amazingly steady light. A century later they provide striking examples of the urge to self-realization as well as almost pure examples of the two poles of the self.

They also exemplify the two sides of the narcissistic character: Wilde the tendency to collapse into enfeeblement when under pressure to sustain grandiose aspirations; Shaw the strength and zeal that can come from identification with ideals when it is supported by a brilliant mind.

As regards their commitment to self-realization, the best way to state it is in their own words. In 'The soul of man under socialism', Wilde wrote: 'the true perfection of man lies, not in what man has but in what man is', and, in the early novel *Immaturity*, Shaw wrote: 'the power to stand alone is worth acquiring at the expense of much sorrowful solitude.' Standing on your own feet and being what you have in you to be are the essentials of individualism.

The lives and personalities of these two men will therefore later be used to provide examples of the two poles of the self, to give some living substance to the concept of the bi-polar self and so to add to our understanding of the developmental process. For the present it is sufficient to say that, when innate talents are great, a stable and creative adjustment may be possible even with total reliance on one or other pole, as would appear to have been the case with Wilde and Shaw. Oscar Wilde's grandiosity and exhibitionism were legendary and, as we shall see later, there are clear indications, both in his developmental history and in his writing, of a disturbance centred on the process of mirroring. Wilde did not live by ideals but purely on immediate experience. As regards Shaw, biographer Holroyd makes abundantly clear not only the importance of idealized values and a strong sense of inner direction, but also the great significance of idealization in Shaw's developmental history. From that idealizing developmental process Shaw constructed an incredibly stable self structure, and from the lives of these two men we can both clarify and confirm the concept of the bi-polar self.

A further strong impetus to the recognition of the clinical relevance of the self came from reading Daniel Stern's *The Interpersonal World of the Infant* which was published in 1985. On the basis of infant observation and research, Stern claimed that there are three developmental levels of the self, and that significant changes in behaviour occur as these levels of self-function emerge. His work and views are the basis of the first chapter which seeks to define the self and its function.

Where he made a particular impact on my journey, however, was in giving further reason for attaching importance to empathy as a relationship dimension of the greatest significance in therapy. As already mentioned, Kohut gave central importance to empathy as a means of data collection and giving definition to the field of psychotherapy. He went further than that, however. In a paper addressed to a community of scholars he referred to empathy as 'the recognition of self in the other' and as 'the accepting and confirming human echo which is an important psychological nutriment'.

The important word here is 'nutriment', because, if accepted, it inevitably gives empathy an important place in the healing process. At the time Kohut proposed this, strong objections were raised from within the psychoanalytic community because it seemed to suggest cure by 'good feelings', and also to undermine both the scientific status of psychoanalysis and one of the basic Freudian tenets: that therapy be carried out in a state of abstinence. Under pressure, Kohut partly withdrew, but he still gave empathic resonance an important place in therapeutic change in his posthumous *How Does Analysis Cure?*

It is here that Stern's work with children is crucial, in that it provides solid ground for the idea of affective attunement between mother and child being a very important psychological nutriment – and affect attunement is an important part of empathy. So this strengthens the claim for empathy's significance in promoting therapeutic change.

Then, at this stage, my attention was drawn to another writer and thinker whose views are congruent with those of Kohut and Lawrence: Martin Buber. For me, his particular importance came from his providing philosophical and empirical evidence for the part played by reciprocity in both the development and the exercise of relationship (and empathy is an important facet and means of reciprocity). Buber distinguished two fundamental ways of relating: I–It and I–Thou. The 'I' of I–Thou is Lawrence's 'I-in-vital centrality'. The relating from that position is intersubjective, and it is of the same nature as Kohut's empathic resonance and Stern's affect attunement. In common terms it is being in tune with the reality of the other person, and it is purely subjective. 'I–It', on the other hand, belongs to the objective world. It is instrumental and self-conscious. Its dynamics are those of separation and possession, of setting apart and using, and the object is always an 'it'.

When Buber looks at the 'I–Thou' of therapy the congruence between his views and Kohut's becomes even more striking. Buber says that therapy can occur only by entering as a partner into a person-to-person relationship, never through the observation and investigation of an object, as psychoanalysis claimed. He suggested that a therapist who is satisfied to analyse his patient may accomplish some repairs, and may help a fragmented self to find some coherence, but cannot fulfil the true task, which is the regeneration of a stunted personal centre. This can be accomplished only by someone who, in Buber's words, 'stands not only at his own pole but also at the other pole, experiencing the effects of his own action', or, in Kohut's terminology, in an ambience of sustained empathic resonance.

Buber is important to us here, however, not only for his contribution to the clinical relevance of the self but also, and perhaps more importantly, because he takes relating into the world of the spirit. He sees 'I–Thou' relating as emerging from the natural association between mother and child, from the intimate togetherness of mother and baby. 'I–It' relating, on the other hand, comes into operation only as some separateness is established.

As each one of the dyad, mother and baby, comes to grips with the separate agency of the other, and mutual respect develops, while the intersubjective I–Thou bond is retained, the natural association changes into a spiritual one as reciprocity and tenderness grow. It is such respectful reciprocity and tenderness, according to Buber, that carries relating into the world of the spirit. He referred to it as 'the current of reciprocity' and regarded it as a spiritual quality of the reality of this world, and not of a separate spiritual domain.

This emphasis on reciprocity, and the intersubjective fit between inner prompting and outer response, takes us back to the grounding of all knowledge in reciprocity, as suggested by Kepler and Lorenz, and to the biological basis of the self which Jung's theory of archetypes provides. Here there is important common ground.

Buber clarifies this further, and in this shows his like-mindedness with Lawrence, by the way he distinguishes egos from persons. Egos, in his view, appear from separation and are concerned with things and with drives (as is Lawrence's 'I-am-I in distinction from a whole universe which is not I'). Persons, on the other hand, appear by entering into relationships with other persons with their whole being, into self-relatedness rather than drive-relatedness; and this is Lawrence's 'I-am-I in vital centrality'. The person says 'I am'; the ego 'This is how I am'. The person relates directly in wholeness; the ego in self-consciousness. The ego does not belong to the current of reciprocity. It is not a natural association into which one's essential being enters spontaneously and freely.

'I–it' relating is always contrived. It is not an 'actuality' (and in saying this Buber is, in a way, suggesting that spiritual relating is more real than objective relating). When man participates in an encounter of reciprocity he meets his Thou and lives in the spirit, and this is the profound and vigorous affirmation that Buber contributes to the concept and importance of empathy, and thus is a bridge built into spirituality.

It is now necessary to make clear what is meant here by spirituality, what view is to be taken. It is a circumscribed and restricted one from which we will start, best approached by stating what it does not entail. It is not a spirituality that involves any particular religious faith or belief, nor is it a spirituality of moral values, such as a sense of the true and the beautiful, nor one of cultural tradition which provides a mythology and defines objects of reverence and awe. We will start simply from the reality of transcendency, in an experiential sense; from the awareness which carries not only a recognition of the immediate and the concrete, but also a sense of the abstract and timeless; the awareness that life cannot be encompassed by rationality but extends into an unknown; and the awareness that certain experiences have a particular quality bringing uplift of spirit. It is a view that Joseph Campbell made central to his understanding of mythology, how phenomenal forms and experiences can become transparencies, revelatory of transcendence. As he wrote in *The Inner Reaches of Outer Space*:

> representing the universe and the whole spectacle of nature, both as known to the mind and beheld by the eye, as an epiphany of such a kind that when lightning flashes, or a setting sun ignites the sky, or a deer is seen standing alerted, the exclamation 'Ah!' may be uttered as a recognition of divinity.

This sparse view of the spiritual is where we begin. However, sparse though it be, it does provide some ground for that other aspect of reality which has probably always been part of what is regarded as the province of the spiritual: the sense of life being a unique journey, which theologian Paul Tillich memorably characterized as 'the courage to be'.

Having opened the perspective on to the spiritual side of life, and given some definition of what is meant by that, it is then easier to make full use of poets and other writers, and in the latter part of the text they will be used to widen the bridge between psychology and spirituality as well as to add substance to the process of therapy. As regards the bridge, the poet Wordsworth will be used to enlarge and enrich the concept of selfobject, taking it well into the spiritual domain.

As regards the process of therapy, and how writers can contribute to this, New Zealand writer Janet Frame will be given pride of place. She was herself a patient in mental hospitals, and exposed to the most awful conditions, for a period of eight years in the 1950s, during which time she had more than two hundred electro-convulsive treatments. From this terrible experience she made a quite remarkable recovery, going on to become a distinguished writer with an international reputation.

She has a special place in my personal journey in that more than twenty years ago I worked at the hospital where she spent most of her patient years. It was then that I developed a strong interest in her truly amazing story, and I feel that this has remained with me, consistently prompting me in what I have pursued. Some of what I have learned from her autobiography and from her novels is introduced here and will be expanded upon later.

In *To the Is-land* Janet Frame writes about the early development of her self. Her early years were largely happy ones, although tinged with the unease of a sensitive self-awareness. She describes her first remembered sense of self, at the age of 3, as a 'burden of sadness and loneliness' which she recognized as being within her, whereas the 'sad song' of the wind was not part of her inner world. In this way she first recognised the separateness of her inner world as the container of the self.

Later in childhood, these early experiences, which gave her self some strength and cohesion, came to full flower, and when the family moved from a situation of isolation to live in a small town she took delight in exploring the new places and having new experiences. Many years later she could describe it all in amazing detail and with remarkable vividness. What comes through in the description is her sense of adventure and wonder, a sense of being vividly alive as a person in the world, and a sense of kinship with other creatures. At these times she felt full of joy and heady anticipation of opportunities for seemingly endless play.

Following this happy period the stone of adversity started to crush her. She began the journey which ended in the hell of her hospital years. She adjusted to the awful events of her adolescence by suppressing her natural liveliness, spontaneity and rebelliousness, while cultivating the world of literature as a safe place for her self and a self-identity as a poet. She created her own selfobject world. Her journey into near-death of the spirit, and her remarkable recovery, will be used to attempt to display the activity of the spirit.

Finally, I want now to return to where we started, and to put what we are considering into a context that highlights and gives urgency to the importance of self-function and the clinical relevance of the self. There is good reason for thinking that, while this is a time when individuality and standing on one's own feet are more than ever an expected condition of existence, the traditional supports of the self are attenuating. This has been strongly suggested by the much respected commentator on literature and language George Steiner. He has drawn attention to the fact that, since the seventeenth century, there has been a major shift from internal to external discourse, and he gives this a special significance because 'the internal modes of self-address may enact absolutely primary and indispensable functions of identity'. He says that, along with a shift to freer expression, notably with women and the under-privileged being allowed a much greater say, and taboo subjects like sex being freed from censorship, there has been 'a marked reduction in those techniques of concentrated internality which went with religious medita-tion, introspection and learning by heart'.

In modern life the emphasis is on external communication, on 'saying it all', 'putting it all out'. In addition, there is the media glut and communication explosion, as well as a huge increase in, and in many an apparent addiction to, external stimulation of all sorts. Steiner suggests that this shift from internal to external discourse, rather than political-economic crises, may be responsible for the anomie and alienation so prevalent at present, and if he is right there would certainly appear to be a big problem indeed. Much greater attention may need to be given to the articulate means of the self, the internal discourse that grounds the self. And, if Zweig is also right, that ours is a time that does not allow the quiet and waiting time necessary for self-collection, then it may be that those of us who are in the business of psychotherapy may have to give much more attention to the conditions of our patients and clients, directing attention to whether they have, or are creating, good conditions for self-restoration. Because, if what we are thinking has some reality to it, it follows that treatments may find their full effectiveness only if the right conditions are present to support psychic growth and healing. And further, with alienation being so much the present norm, and also the main block to the true reciprocity which is the self's life-blood, major changes may be needed to the process and aims of psychotherapy.

This account of my journey forms the basis on which we will proceed, with the focus being the clinical relevance of the self and the aim to get to a clearer understanding of the psyche on which to ground more effective therapy. The aim, and the claim, is that this can be therapy of both self and spirit. It is offered in the hope of its being a guide to further exploration and encouraging others to attempt the journey. It is but a guide, and no attempt will be made at comprehensiveness nor will all avenues that are opened be explored. Directions will be suggested, signposts erected, evidence offered, leaving readers ample room in which to make their own journey in reciprocity with the text.

Chapter 1

The self in being

To get to grips with understanding self-function it is necessary to begin with a technical discussion of what constitutes the self and how the self develops, and for many this may prove to be the most difficult part of the task before us. A large part of the difficulty lies in the fact that the self is purely subjective. In ordinary awareness we live in an objective world, a world that we experience as 'out there'. In order to grasp the self we have to change perspective, to use sense and imagination to contact pure subjectivity, and it is something that requires effort because it does not come naturally. Another part of the difficulty comes from the fact that much subjectivity lies outside conscious awareness. But this is simply to state the problem. Solutions can be found only by going into the technicalities and by making the necessary imaginative effort.

During the last two decades a revolution in infancy research and observation has been occurring. This has demonstrated that the infant has capacities which previously had not been imagined possible, and also that what can be regarded as self-function develops very early. In his seminal book *The Interpersonal World of the Infant* Daniel Stern presented some of this work and made it the basis of his suggestion that there are four distinct senses of self which emerge successively during infancy, and that these developments are marked by changes occurring in how an infant behaves and relates. The following exposition is largely based on Stern.

The first notable change occurs at the age of two months when the infant begins to make eye contact, shortly afterwards starts to smile and coo more frequently and then appears not only to enjoy interacting but also to initiate it. Stern suggests that this transformation indicates the emergence of a core sense of self, and that over the next few months this is consolidated into a subjective sense of being a separate, cohesive, bounded physical unit with a sense of agency, affectivity and continuity in time. A sense of self-definition has developed. 'I am' may be said to have been born, and during the time this is happening, between two and six months, the infant appears to demonstrate an increasing sense of self-possession and an awareness of other people as separate beings. This profound change, clearly recognized by mothers, raises the question of what changes occur in the infant to bring it about. It also questions the significance of consciousness because it happens long before there can be any consciousness of self.

These are the sorts of questions that new research has been attempting to answer. The following examples of experiments with and observation of infants are given simply to provide some idea of how this has been done.

1 Of fundamental importance was the observation that infants regularly occupy a state when they are quiet and alert, and at such times are apparently taking in the external world. Such states of alert inactivity can last for several minutes and provide an opportunity for doing tests. They provide a window to look through.

2 Head turning can be used at such times to test a new-born's ability to discriminate. It has been used to show that 3-day-old infants can discriminate the smell of their own mother's milk. When mother's breast pad was placed on one side, and a pad from another nursing mother placed on the other, babies regularly turned towards their own mother's pad.

3 Experiments have demonstrated that a baby can transfer sensual experience from one modality to another. This would appear to be happening when a baby grasping an object uses vision to determine the hand size necessary for a particular object. Pacifiers with nipples of different shapes were used to test this. Babies were allowed to suck one of the nipples, while blindfolded, and subsequently, when this nipple was placed alongside one of a different shape, the babies, after visual inspection, looked more frequently at the one they had just sucked, the one it seemed they 'knew' from their sucking experience and could identify visually.

4 Different experiments have demonstrated dramatically a baby's capacity to act as its own agent. The sucking reflex can be used for this too, and infants can be rapidly trained to suck to get something to happen. If an electrically bugged nipple, connected to the starter mechanism of a tape-recorder, is placed in the infant's mouth, the infant will soon suck at the rate to get the sound it wants, and will show apparent pleasure in doing so.

These are but a few examples of a rapidly developing area of research which indicates that, rather than being the *tabula rasa* on which experience makes its imprint to mould the person, as was at one time thought, the baby from the start of life takes its own initiatives and asserts its own capacities. A strong motivation to order the universe seems to be present from the very beginning, and not only is this an inner-driven urge but it is one that appears to be innately satisfying. The joy of self-actualization is apparently present from the start of life.

Stern further suggests that, prior to the establishment of the sense of core self, there is, from birth, the sense of an emergent self. Essentially he means by this that the infant can 'experience' the process of emerging organization, and this is what he calls the emergent sense of self. To support this view he uses the baby's capacity to transfer perceptual experience from one sensory modality to another, and the evidence that babies experience persons as unique from the start, as when a 3-day-old appears to discriminate and imitate smiles, frowns and surprise facial expressions.

A difficulty we may have with this view, and it is a difficulty we will have throughout the exploration of the self, is knowing what is meant here by 'experience'. As we live so much in the realm of consciousness, and clear consciousness can come to define knowing, experience comes to be tied to what we are aware of consciously. In other words, in this view knowing something means being conscious of it. But the fact is that a great deal of 'knowing' goes on at a non-conscious level, and much of it cannot be translated into consciousness at all. So what is this sense of emergent self that is experienced? Certainly it has no consciousness attached. It is purely subjective and it cannot be made objective. It is pre-conceptual. However, all that happens in life 'exists' in the existential sense, and all that happens is registered in organic being, and is registered in the being of the baby subsequently to alter behaviour. To that extent, and that extent only, is it 'experienced', and we need continually to remind ourselves that consciousness plays only a very small part in existential experience. Its overriding presence tends to dominate thinking, however, making it hard to think of experience as not bearing on consciousness. And we also need to keep in mind that it is this type of experience which has little bearing on consciousness that is the essence of selfobject experience.

It is with the sense of core self that we get on to what feels like firmer ground, although again this is happening long before consciousness is in operation. Experiences that are available to the infant from which a sense of self can develop, and which give some concrete substance to selfhood, are:

1 *Self-agency, in the sense of being author of one's own actions* and making expected consequences happen. It is easy to imagine what an exciting and fundamentally important discovery it must be to find that by one's own actions pleasurable experiences can be made to last, and a baby of a few weeks is discovering that.
2 *Self-coherence* in the way of having a consistent sense of intactness within a boundary. Perhaps it requires a more sustained imaginative exercise to picture how this may slowly emerge.
3 *Self-affectivity* as inner feelings (such as joy, interest, distress, surprise and anger, with their characteristic pattern and tone of pleasure–displeasure) repeatedly occur, and become attached to other self-experience.
4 *Self-history* with the sense of continuity into the past and into present on-goingness.

These experiences on their own, but more particularly when they operate together and become linked, provide 'islands of consistency' from which the core self gradually grows and is consolidated. It is from daily life events, particularly of social interaction, and most particularly in contact with the primary care-giver, that the infant identifies the invariants of experience which build a core self and, complementarily, those that specify an 'other'.

As regards agency, some sense of volition is probably present from soon after birth. As intense interactions increase, with the fine capacity the infant has for recognizing pattern it comes to sense that some of what is experienced is the consequence of its own actions (a limb moves when wanted; closing eyes brings darkness; turning head makes things move) and some are not. Some of the latter come to be recognized as caused by a particular other, especially the presence of mother. However, it is the sense of self-agency operating in innumerable repetitions of affectively charged experiences which provides the main grounding of the self.

The self can be said to be born out of affect. Registration of these repetitive experiences coalesces as a result of the infant's capacity for integrated memory. It would seem that infants have the ability to aggregate experiences and distil an average prototype, and such representations form the basic units of the core self. 'Nursing with mother', 'playing with mother', 'soothing myself' are examples of the abstract representations formed in this way, making 'islands of consistency', the seeds from which the core self grows.

Another feature these representations are thought to have is that, once they are established, they have, as part of their nature, the sense of being-with-someone, which sense is present in the experiences when-ever and however they are evoked. The nursing experience is of the greatest significance in this and, with the repetition of its regular pattern, it comes to have a memorial representation which aggregates all parti-cular experiences of being fed. When this is established, then, whenever and however the representation of nursing with mother is evoked, mother is experienced as present whether she actually is or not, and such inner representations form the supportive substance of the self. They are purely subjective, and although they result from interactions with external objects they are not the reality of those interactions but abstrac-tions from them. Such basic relationship experiences which evoke and nurture the self we have come to know as selfobject experiences.

We have already noted the importance that will be attached to the concept of selfobject, and some definition of it has been given. This will be expanded later, but for the present let it be defined metaphorically by saying that the core self is the seed and selfobject experience the soil – soil that is the nourishing ground of the self; soil that belongs to the self and on which the self is dependent, although there is as little recognition of the dependence as there is of the need for oxygen until the supply is reduced; and soil that is necessary throughout life. Self Psychology has moved away from making independence the goal of psychological development and from regarding dependence as immature. Having a mature dependence is the very ground of independent action and autonomy.

The next notable change in the sense of self occurs during the period between seven and sixteen months when communication becomes established between mother and child. From this the child develops the sense of having a mind, an inner state of being, an inner world which can communicate with others. Communication is at first by gesture, posture and facial expression, with a few sounds. Such non-verbal communi-cation can be very precise in meaning, however, and effective in results. By such means the infant learns to communicate intention or desire ('I want you to attend to me') or to direct a focus of attention ('look at this toy'). When this happens successfully, a new organizing dimension of the self emerges: intersubjectivity becomes operative and is the second main stage of development of the self. Core relatedness establishes the physical and sensory distinction of the self and other. Intersubjective relatedness adds the internal subjective states which lie behind the behaviour, and which can also interact. How mother and baby experience each other comes to be part of their interaction, and the two crucial areas in which this at first occurs are in sharing a focus of attention – as when a child directs mother's attention to a toy with which they then play – and in sharing wishes and intentions – as when mother holds something the infant wants and encourages the child to reach and grasp for it. In such ways a well-functioning mother–child couple not only learns to interact and play together but also to bring the best out of each other, and learning how to do that is extremely important in any relationship including the therapeutic relationship. Therapy, too, can be seen as a relationship process which moves towards each bringing the best out of the other, when it is going well.

There is, however, another area of intersubjectivity to which Stern gives particular significance and that is the sharing of affective states. He suggests that such sharing results in a particular phenomenon: 'affect attunement'. He gives this great importance both in the development of the self and in understanding the therapeutic process. Affect attunement occurs when a mother accurately reads an episode of the child's behaviour as it expresses a feeling state, and adapts her behavioural response to it. In doing so mother does not simply imitate the behaviour of the child but matches her response in terms of intensity (level of arousal) and shape (crescendo or diminuendo). Thus, if the child goes into a state of increasing excitement over a new experience, mother matches this verbally by following the changing pattern of the child's behaviour with the changing expressions of her voice. When this happens, sharing of affective states occurs as a special form of communication, and there is experimental evidence that such affect attunement can be both a soothing and a strengthening experience for the child. It is thought to promote the growth of the self, and that its absence can be disruptive and damaging to the self.

When intersubjectivity is established, empathy is no longer a process that goes on unnoticed. It enters awareness as a sense of there being a bridge between two minds. Psychic intimacy, the sharing of one's inner being, then becomes a possibility. Such sharing, of which affect attunement is a particular form, comes to have great importance as development proceeds. It may not be an exaggeration to say that the desire to know and be known, in the sense of mutually revealing subjective experience, begun at this early stage, may well be a dominating influence throughout the rest of life. It may be the deepest of human yearnings, and its absence the greatest of human lacks. What is amazing, if current thinking is right, is that it becomes established so early.

With the emergence of language, during the second year of life, the sense of self takes on new attributes which also prove momentous. The fourth stage of development of the self, the verbal self, is reached. The use of symbols allows an objective view of self to emerge: 'this is me' experience becomes a dawning reality (long after the 'I am' of the core self); the use of personal pronouns begins; the subjective–objective dichotomy, which can so confuse comprehension, is established. And somewhere, amidst all this, consciousness first dawns, and it is of the utmost importance to be aware of how much development of the self has occurred before the appearance of consciousness. It is important for an understanding of human nature. It is particularly important for therapists to keep in mind.

The period of formation of the verbal self is thought to be from about eighteen to thirty months. Prior to this infants do not seem to know that what they see in a mirror is their own reflection. After about eighteen months they do. Also the capacity for symbolic play emerges then, and shows that the child can begin to comprehend quite complex social situations. In this way the sense of verbal self, a labelled self existing in a social context, is established.

The introduction of language not only changes the internal world of the child but also greatly changes self–other relatedness. It enhances communication and the sharing of a personal world. It adds a new dimension to the sense of personal continuity. It introduces the ability to narrate one's own life story in the context of a family to which one belongs. The child can now say to itself: 'This is me as I was and am and this is my family', and thus develops an abstracted sense of 'me-ness' with which he or she can interact, and negotiate, and pursue the search for meaning in relation to the 'you-ness' of mother and others.

It can be said that with the establishment of the verbal self the foundations of personhood have been fully laid, and this has happened by the age of 2. The acquisition of language is, however, not an unmixed blessing. The new level of relatedness resulting from the use of words does not eclipse what has previously operated. It is of the essence of self-function that established levels are not replaced by the new but continue to operate along with the new. Core relatedness and inter-subjective relatedness continue, and from this universe of non-verbal experience language takes hold of a part and transforms it. Sometimes language captures what is quintessential and then can be profoundly meaningful in a personal sense, can add a new dimension to 'truth'. Often, however, it can grasp only a part. Furthermore, some global experiences at the level of core or subjective relatedness are probably not susceptible to representation in words or, if they are, only in the language of poetry. Because of this, language both enhances and frag-ments experience; both promotes mutual understanding and, by dis-tancing from immediate experience, creates alienation. And when to this is added the ability to distort and misrepresent, the two-edged nature of the sword of language is clear. From this perspective, too, the spiritual advantages of core and subjective relatedness, present in more primitive stages of human development, are apparent. The yearning to return to nature and to the Eden of innocence, which can be such a powerful pull, may be a yearning to get back not simply to the safety and comfort of the womb but to a more spiritual sense of togetherness. Attunement is more than communication. It is communion.

From this outline of the developmental stages of the self we can now briefly look at the clinical implications. Intersubjective relating (which is such an important advance) adds the extra dimension of mutual sharing and influence on each other of two subjectivities to the purely sensual state of core relatedness (which from the infant's side can be categorized as life in the presence of a self-regulating other). It is a shift to attunement which allows the care-taker to be able to influence the subjectivity of the child, and here may be the genesis of many future problems. A baby could not survive radical failure at the earliest stages, and complete non-attunement is probably so rare as to have little significance. However, because mothers attempt to have some influence on their off-spring, and use their responses to do this, selective attunement is the norm, and it is here that things can start to go wrong. Selective responsiveness is an important part of the socializing process. Good behaviour is rewarded. Bad behaviour gets a negative or no response. With this, however, comes the possibility of both moving the child away from its own nature, with the creation of a 'false self', as well as the possibility of exclusion of certain experiences from intersubjective sharing. Regarding the latter, and to quote Stern:

> Whatever happens next, whether the experience excluded from the interpersonal sphere becomes part of the 'false-self' or 'not me' phenomenon, whether it is simply relegated out of consciousness, one way or another, or whether it remains a private but accessible part of the self, the beginning [of failure to integrate one's whole nature] lies here.

This is the first point of origin of disorders and divisions of the self.

Misattunement is another possibility that can have far-reaching consequences. Misattunement offers an unfitting response in order to discourage the child's particular behaviour, rather than simply choosing not to respond as in selective attunement. Doing this may not necessarily be damaging but if it is excessive there can only be erosion of the innate being of the child as it is denied the matching confirmation of mother's responses.

Worse than misattunement is when mother (and the term mother is being used to include any consistent care-taker) deliberately enters the child's world and then uses power and position to change the child. This is the mother who says 'I know you better than you know yourself'. The only option for the child may then be to learn devious ways of keeping intact their own subjective reality, which is likely to lead to later asocial behaviour. In these and other ways the grounds of future psycho-pathology can be formed at a very early age.

Failure of the process of mirroring, of which affect attunement is an important part, is now given an important place in the clinical perception of the development of pathology. Looking at Stern's view of the process of mirroring operating at three levels is a way of reviewing the develop-mental stages of the self. The three levels are:

1   Behavioural responsivity and regulation at the core level. Mother and child are in contact in a purely sensual way in which mother plays a regulating part.
2   Attunement in its many forms and expressions at the intersubjective level.
3   Reinforcement, shaping and consensual validation of experience and behaviour at the verbal level.

Essentially, mirroring is a process that confirms and consolidates the child's innate and true-self being.

Selective attunement and misattunement may have clinical con-sequences, but a mother's ability actually to change the infant's emotional experience can be even more damaging. One way this can happen is by mother repeatedly and consistently disconfirming the child's emotions, and this most commonly occurs in relation to 'bad' feelings. If, when the child is sulking or angry, mother consistently responds in a disapproving manner that matches the arousal level of the child, then it is likely that such affects will in time attenuate and be lost from the child's affective repertoire. In this way children are produced who are unable to have bad feelings. Not only fall-out from disconfirmation, but also actual changing of affective response is possible, as when mother does not comfort a child in distress but shakes the child out of it by forcibly introducing something exciting. Long-standing disabilities can result from such transactions when they are per-sistently repeated, and being at a pre-verbal level they can be impenetrable to change.

Finally, Stern suggests that, in addition to an understanding of the different levels of self-functioning, and how they are responded to, contributing to formulations about psychopathology, they can also lead to better therapeutic strategies: 'the notion of a layering of different senses of the self as different forms of experience is potentially helpful in locating an organizing therapeutic metaphor.' What he means by therapeutic metaphor is a statement that encapsulates in a meaningful way the essence of the problem, which can then be used as a focus of therapy. Material from a patient's current life situation, as well as from reactions to the therapist, will usually indicate which sense of self carries most of the damage – whether it is the core self, where physical agency and control is the main issue, or the intersubjective level, where feeling states and intentions are what matter most, or at the verbal level where words are dominant.

Two important therapeutic consequences can result from recognizing which domain of the self is predominantly involved in a person's psychopathology. First, it can help to clarify where it all began, which can strengthen the therapeutic metaphor and lead to further insight. Second, it can help to get in touch with the affect that has been blocked. Sometimes the crucial issue is clear to both therapist and patient, but the patient cannot get in touch with the feelings involved. The key affect is not available because it has suffered the fate of attenuation, and recognizing the crucial self-function involved can sometimes open the door.

An example is needed to make this clearer. Mary J, who had always been a strong, self-reliant person, the care-taker in her family and later a nurse, collapsed into a chronic pain syndrome and severe depression following an operation on her lumbar spine. She was aware that she had a problem with dependency, tending to be independent to a fault, and that this was contributing to her difficulties. But it was not clear why her collapse had been so complete. After a time she reluctantly revealed that her father had walked out on the family a short time after her birth, which raised the likelihood that this was where it all began, that it was at the core self her problems lay. This was supported by the fact that she was very good in the intersubjective and verbal domains, good at dealing with empathic failures and with talking things out in her professional role. The recognition of the key importance of the core self, with its embeddednes in physical agency, also provided an explanation for the observation that she was much more at ease when talking about what was wrong with her body than about emotions and her mental state. The body was where the energy lay, and when there was mutual understanding that her vulnerability lay particularly in the area of physical agency, and it was because of this vulnerability that she had collapsed so badly, the door was opened to a much fuller exploration, which previously she had resisted. Her self-blaming diminished but the real

pay-off came when she got hold of the key affect: the extreme humiliation she felt at not being able to mobilize herself.

Thus an understanding of the different levels of self-experience can
help the process of therapy. It can also help to specify what is needed of
the therapist. At the core level, attunement requires a sense of physical
presence. Seeing the physical presence of the therapist may be
sufficient, but not infrequently it also includes a pressing need for
merging and for some physical contact. As the latter may come to be
sexualized it can present a difficult problem for the therapist, being
either a potential hazard or a potential disjunction, as the therapist is
either drawn into sexual contact or adopts too distant a posture in order
to be safe.

At the intersubjective level it is particularly the need for attunement
in a non-verbal way that is supreme. Not just seeing and being seen in a
physical sense but a 'seeing into' and a sharing in the area of affects and
intentions. This is what Kohut describes as empathic resonance, and it
requires that both participants be responsively alive and attuned to each
other. Finally, at the verbal level, it is being engaged in the reciprocity
of words that makes for effective therapy: being able to put into words
what is 'seen into'; using words for effective communication, and to
create the metaphors and narratives that form the heart of the therapeutic
process.

Such is the contribution that infant observation and research is
making to an understanding of self-function, as well as to an understanding of both disorder of the self and some of the requirements of
therapy. The main contribution so far made to the clinical application of
Self Psychology is in extending and making more precise the concepts
of empathic resonance and of mirroring, subjects which will be taken up
in the next chapter. It is likely, however, that these are only the first
fruits, and that further work in this area may make a major contribution
to developments in psychotherapy and in the understanding of
relationship.

Chapter 2

The self in action

There are three ways in which we can examine the self in action, and these will be taken in turn although they all operate together and are simply different ways of looking at the whole.

The first aspect is the essential nature of the self, and it is here that the distinction between true self and false self operates. Being true to . oneself is a possibility that is generally accepted, although it is difficult to define precisely what is meant by the phrase, while at the same time knowing well in one's heart what it means (such is the reality of subjectivity). It can be said that it is being true to one's essential being, to authentic inner directedness, and it is implicit in the theory of the self that the neonate is born with certain potentials that are part of its biological heritage, one of which is the emergence of a sense of self-hood. This sense of selfhood carries its own emerging directedness and it is this that determines authenticity. It is to this inner directedness that one can be true or false.

It is much easier to be clear about false-self function because it can be dealt with objectively. False-self function is thinking and behaviour that is determined by compliance to external pressure. What comes naturally to a child may not be what parents and others in authority want of the child, and it is as the child complies with pressures to be and do what others expect, in ways that are not part of its own nature, that a false self develops. Of course it is possible to comply on the surface while keeping intact an inner sense of self that knows what is true and what is not. This means that, should circumstances change to allow behaviour that is natural and spontaneous to flourish, then it can happen. Once started, this can be a continuing process which can last a lifetime if inner strength and conviction grow, if one remains in touch with one's essential being and if outer constraints allow. Starting this process of true-self becoming can be one of the results of therapy, and one of the advantages of old age may be that, freed from having to comply in work situations or under family and social pressure, one can just 'be oneself' to an extent that was never possible previously.

When compliance has been extreme, however, it is possible that true-self sense may be lost for all practical purposes. False-self functioning and experience then come to dominate the personality, even to the extent that recognition that this is so may also be lost. Nevertheless, it is likely that, even at this extreme, the spark of true self does not die completely, and this is something that can be picked up empathically as one gets to know a person in some depth, in therapy or otherwise. People can 'know' in their hearts that there is something within they have lost, while denying it in their actions and statements about themselves. Getting in touch with that is a very important part of therapeutic work.

A child cannot survive without some sense of acceptance, and if this can only be bought by compliance, and in the process there is little recognition and acceptance of the child's essential being, then a false self grows. Once the process has started it tends to gain its own momentum as the child learns how acceptance is earned and maintained. The rewards of this are not only the experience of being acceptable, and of thus being supported, which is so vital to the child, but also that of having some power in life, albeit at a big price. In this way great social skill and high achievement can develop, but at the cost of increasing alienation from the essential self, and in the end this can prove fatal. For it would appear that being in touch with one's essential self is a crucially important source of natural vitality. There is every reason for thinking that, in addition to biological drive, the true self is a potent source of motivation and energy, as seen when in a playful or in a creative spell. When this is no longer available, when the inner spark is lost, then enfeeblement and collapse can occur. This is a likely outcome in even successful false-self adaptations. It is also frequently an aspect of mid-life crisis when, having achieved the social and personal goals that society ordains, the issue of self-being is faced, but inner direction and conviction are lacking, and vitality is not there.

There is a fundamental problem in this aspect of development which it is important to recognize. Being true to oneself means standing apart, standing on one's own feet, being separate; sustaining a sense of self, on the other hand, requires a feeling of belonging, requires not only the experience of being held and nurtured but also some sense of being part of and in tune with one's experiential world, and it is the latter need that prompts compliance. The fundamental contrariness in these needs – to be both distinct from and embedded within one's experiential world – is difficult to resolve. Certain personality types can be seen as resulting from failure to make such a resolution. At one extreme is the narcissistic person who creates and projects a sense of self-distinction but comes to feel increasingly alienated, and at the other extreme the excessively dependent person who is well embedded but lacks self-assertion. In between are all possible variations, all of them attempts to resolve the contrary needs for attachment and separation, for independence and belonging, for self-assertion and for social integration. These polarities can be seen as defining one of life's most important tasks: achieving individuality without alienation.

The second way of looking at the self is in terms of its immediate function. The self cannot function in a vacuum but only within a matrix of selfobject experience, and its cohesion, strength and vitality are determined by the vicissitudes of these experiences. This is the basic fact of the self and underlies all understanding of self-function. Therefore, understanding selfobject experience is crucial to understanding the self, and some repetition may be necessary in the process of doing so. A selfobject experience is any experience that functions to evoke the structured self (which becomes manifest to the experiencing individual as a sense of one's own selfhood) or to maintain the continuity of such selfhood. While these experiences are related to objects, be they people or things, they are not the actuality of those relationships but their internal reflection. They are purely subjective. Selfobject experience occurs in the self's inner space and creates its inner space. With constant repetition selfobject experiences create an inner world which is a reflection of the outer, and the result of this is that in time the inner world becomes self-sustaining so that dependence on the outer world is lessened. This can explain how certain people can have a lot of strength of spirit and yet have little in the way of external support. Their internal world is so rich that it is sufficient.

In the beginning, however, dependency can only be great. The infant needs not only certainty of the presence of the person who functions as a selfobject, the primary care-giver, but also a sense of being in possession and control of the experience, which at that stage means the object itself. This is the illusion of omnipotence the infant needs to sustain the emerging self. In the beginning selfobjects are experienced as belonging to and under control of the self, and under favourable circumstances they facilitate the acquisition of normal grandiosity and exhibitionism (the infant who struts with delight when showing off a newly acquired skill). They allow for delight in the self which is a normal and necessary part of healthy narcissism. In time, however, the differentiation of self and other requires relinquishment of the early sense of omnipotence, and, when this has happened, selfobjects are then experienced as conditional containers, confirmers, supporters and extenders of the self. No longer under fantasied omnipotent control they become part of the living world of the self which the child learns to manipulate to provide a continuing sense of intactness and hope.

Very early selfobject needs are referred to as archaic and, where there have been significant deficiencies at this early stage, the resulting self-deficits are great. They may be covered over only to re-emerge in the stresses of later relationships, and this frequently happens in intensive therapy. When it does, the patient may then demand either omnipotent control over the therapist or that the therapist be all-knowing and all-powerful, something we will look at in more detail later.

In normal development, however, as time goes by, and selfobject sustainment has created the foundations of an inner world, the dependency lessens. A 2-year-old may play alone for some time apparently oblivious of mother's presence or absence (although careful observation may note brief glances to check that she is there) but becomes unsettled if mother moves to another room. As the months go by, the periods of separation can be longer without causing distress to the child. To some extent this process can be understood in terms of attachment behaviour; that is, as a biological phenomenon. But more than that would seem to be involved. Winnicott observed how children use particular objects (blankets, pieces of cloth, toys) as a source of security, and become distressed if they are not available. He referred to these as transitional objects, as they are objects of the real world but have acquired a private symbolic meaning for the child. Therefore it would seem that, in addition to biologically based attachment, the child develops from selfobject experience an inner world of memories and symbols which can then be used to reduce dependency on actual relationships.

In adolescence, children become disillusioned with parents and turn away from intimacy with them, looking elsewhere for selfobject needs. Peer relationships become particularly intense; belonging to a group or gang becomes important; particular values and ideals are adopted; conformity to group mores becomes strong. All these can be seen as particular manoeuvres that are necessary during a period of major selfobject adjustment. The inner world is still there but its anchorage in the outer world is under major reconstruction.

In adult life, selfobject experience is still as necessary but its form greatly changes. Marriage and parenthood provide roles that have a self-sustaining function. Expansion of self boundaries to include spouse and children allows participation in the self-sustaining selfobject experience of others, as if it were the self. Work and friends provide a wider selfobject ambience. But also selfobject experience becomes more abstract and symbolic. Reading a novel, listening to music, meditation, communing with nature can all take on a self-sustaining function as the inner world is cultivated and becomes ever more important as a means of maintaining the self. With the satisfactory development of this process comes greater internal strength.

So far, in this discussion of selfobject experience, it would appear that the self is largely the passive recipient of some action of the selfobject. In Chapter 1, however, we saw how active the infant is in taking initiatives and in ordering its world, and this probably applies to selfobject experience as well. The observation that infants actually experience pleasure when they have contingent control over external events has led some to suggest that awareness of bringing about desired results, and the pleasurable sense of efficacy that goes with that, are actual foundations of self-feeling. Be that as it may, there is every reason for thinking that a sense of agency, not only in external activity but also in creation of the inner world, is a very important part of the function of the self. The effectiveness of this may result from both taking the necessary initiatives and from doing so in an imaginative way. Indeed, it may not be too far from reality to think that being imaginatively creative, in the widest sense, is the self's primary propensity and task.

In development, the self grows strong and functions effectively only when in an ambience of selfobject experience. This also applies in an immediate way. Fluctuations in how people respond to one can rapidly affect confidence and energy. Speaking in public is a situation in which these effects can be striking. If the audience remains alert and interested, and particularly if acclaim and appreciation are shown, then the speaker feels encouraged and energized, and is likely to perform well. If, on the other hand, people are restless and look bored, then the speaker is likely to suffer a steady deflation, and may have to struggle to finish the address. Such is the effect of audience response, and such is the nature of selfobject experience as it continuously influences the functional state of the self.

The third aspect of the self to be considered is the structural, and this involves a fundamental concept of Self Psychology: the bi-polar self. This is a spatial metaphor Kohut used to represent the recognition that there are two different types of selfobject experience, from which two particular parts, or 'poles', of self-structure are precipitated. One pole results from mirroring selfobject experiences, and is referred to as the pole of ambitions; the other emerges from idealizing selfobject experiences and is referred to as the pole of values and ideals. Mirroring is the experience of self-reflection; idealizing the experience of feeling part of something bigger and stronger (which may ultimately include feelings of patriotism or being a valued member of a political party or church). Mirroring meets needs for affirmation and confirmation; idealizing for feeling part of something which is admired and has calming and protective qualities. Prototypically, mirroring is the gleam in mother's observing eye; idealizing is being calmed and strengthened in mother's arms. As a result of the validation of self by the process of mirroring, childish grandiosity and exhibitionism (the proudly strutting infant saying 'look how great I am') are ultimately transformed into mature self-assertion, ambition and solid self-esteem. The soothing and strengthening experiences of idealization ultimately produce idealized values and internalized guiding principles.

From this polarity comes the basic duality of the 'being' self at the exhibitionist pole, which puts high value on spontaneity and immediate experience, and the 'doing' self at the idealizing pole, which values work and achievement most highly. Ernest Wolf, a colleague of Kohut's, has suggested that dominance of the 'being' pole produces the 'charismatic'-type person, while dominance of the 'doing' pole is characteristic of 'messianic' personalities. In the harmoniously balanced self, which theoretically should be the ideal, ambitious extension of the self would be modulated and controlled by firm guidance from internal standards, and natural spontaneity would provide some relief from tendencies to perfectionism and driving oneself too hard. There is, however, no such being as an ideal person, but only endless variability and variations of successful and unsuccessful adaptations to life's demands and opportunities.

When natural talents are very great, then balance is certainly of much less significance, and we can see in Oscar Wilde and G.B. Shaw striking examples of highly creative people who were nevertheless 'unbalanced' in having marked dominance of one pole of the self. Indeed, they can be seen as almost pure examples of the poles of the self, and therefore can be used to fill out our conception of the bi-polar self. In Oscar Wilde's early years, the search for self-realization, a central theme throughout his life which undoubtedly had a grandiose quality, found expression in aesthetic and behavioural extravagance. Immediate experience was what mattered to him, and the policy of living he adopted was one of going from one exciting sensation to another. He wished to make his life a work of art, and this led him to the view that sin is more useful to society than martyrdom, sin being self-expressive and not self-repressive. Only through free expression is art possible, and Wilde made that his style of living. However, in the end, this non-judgemental pursuit of sensual experience, supported by the contemporary cult of decadence, as his biographer Richard Ellmann puts it, 'summoned him to an underground life totally at variance with his above-board role as Constance's husband'. His life fell apart in narcissistic excess.

In this way Wilde was characteristic of the 'being' person who puts the highest value on immediate experience. He also had the characteristic features of the 'charismatic' type. He easily charmed people and was at his most creative when he had an audience. W.H. Auden said of him that he was a performer rather than a writer, and all the many eminent people who knew him seemed to agree that he could captivate any audience, and that the more response he had the better he performed. If this was so, it provides interesting evidence to support the Self Psychology view of the strengthening and energizing effects of mirroring selfobjects, and the need of a feeble self system to seek constant mirroring.

In what is known of Wilde's developmental years, there is evidence to support the view that there was some deficiency in the process of mirroring. His mother was a very strong and rather domineering person. She is reported to have said that she wished to rage through life, that orthodox creeping was too tame for her. Oscar was Lady Wilde's second son, and she was thought to be bitterly disappointed he was not a girl. It was also said that she expected great things of Oscar.

In his formulation of the relationship between Wilde and Lord Alfred Douglas as the Overloved meeting the Underloved, Auden suggested that, because of the all-possessing love of Lady Wilde, Oscar did not have the experience of deserving love in his own right. If this was so, then his mirroring could only have been defective, and because of Lady Wilde's expectations, particularly in the early years, his individuality may have received little validation and confirmation, which could have been why he was always seeking an audience.

Supporting these suggestions of a developmental disturbance of the process of mirroring is the fact that the mirroring theme is frequently present in Oscar Wilde's writing, perhaps most dramatically in *The Picture of Dorian Gray* (in which the portrait carries the reflection and the burden of the truth of Dorian), but also present in his other stories. The special value given to the mirror appears in 'The Fisherman and his Soul', in which, on the soul's first journey, in the temple is found the Mirror of Wisdom which is worshipped as God. In 'The Star Child', the grandiose child in the end sees his reality, his ugliness, in the water of the well, and then goes in search of the mother he had spurned. And Wilde has his own story of Narcissus, the essence of which is that when Narcissus died the flowers asked the river for drops of water to weep with, but the river could not spare any because it loved him so much. The flowers said: 'How could you not [see how] he was so beautiful?' The river replied: 'If I loved him it was because whenever he leaned over the bank and looked into me I saw the reflection of my waters in his eye.' There could be no lovelier or clearer description of the process of mirroring than this, and there is a particular poignancy about it if we are right in thinking of what was lacking in mother's reflection.

The importance of idealization in Shaw's personal development and function is made explicitly and abundantly clear by his biographer Michael Holroyd. It is also present in what Shaw has to say about himself. He wrote of his father:

> the wrench from childish faith . . . as perfect and omnipotent to the discovery that he was a hypocrite and a dipsomaniac was so sudden and violent that it must have left its mark on me.

From then on he saw his father through his mother's critical eyes, and modelled himself on the opposite of his father. Meanwhile his mother made him miserable by neglect. He could do nothing to interest her, and that neither of his parents seemed to care for him taught him the value of independence and self-sufficiency. By a policy of attracting from the world the attention he had been denied by his mother he, as Holroyd succinctly puts it, 'conjured optimism out of deprivation'. And, despite her lack of interest, his mother apparently came to be a focus for his idealization. Shaw wrote of her: 'I could idolize her to the utmost pitch of my imagination having no sordid or disillusioning contacts with her to correct this.' In this way was Shaw's self made. He created the idealized image of what he wanted to be from the reverse of his father, and used his mother as a fantasied approving presence as a support. Not only did this not require supportive mirroring, it was a structure of complete detachment, having no relationship ground, not at least until a third person entered the picture, the remarkable George Lee.

Lee was an incredible man who coaxed people into doing things beyond their natural powers, and whose ambitions were without limit. He entered Mrs Shaw's life when she joined his musical society and became a devotee of his method of teaching singing. Later, he was to form a *ménage à trois* with the Shaws. It was considered a possibility that he may have been Shaw's actual father, and in a photograph in which they are both present there is a strong resemblance between them, but it is more likely that Shaw simply had a subconscious wish to be the son of this remarkable man. He came to model himself on Lee and adopted many of his startling ideas. Lee was the superman Shaw latched on to and later, when Lee went on to conquer the musical world of London as he had done that of Dublin, with Mrs Shaw following, George Bernard Shaw followed as well, intent on fulfilling the call of his secret self to greatness.

He began the ascent by being Lee's amanuensis. Later on he repeatedly got involved in triangular relationships which seemed to be chaste versions of Lee's relationship with his parents. It would appear that he had actively to deny the possibility of a romantic attachment between Lee and his mother, and that these relationships were enactments which helped confirm this denial. And, as a final feature of this complex process of self-creation by idealization, and making best use of what was available to him, Shaw probably used his mother as a model as well as a fantasied supporting presence. If he could not be a person to attract her attention, he could at least become the sort of person she was, as Holroyd puts it, 'insensible to public opinion and a Bohemian without Bohemian vices'.

These two men provide very clear representations of the differences between mirroring and idealizing selfobjects, and they clearly show how the former are relationship-bound and the latter relationship-independent. Insensibility to public opinion and lack of need for personal acclaim as well as for personal relationships, while at the same time attracting public attention in a Bohemian way, was certainly characteristic of Shaw. He worked and lived in detachment. He did not need to be liked or loved, and Oscar Wilde said of him that he was a man with no enemies but not even his friends liked him. Wilde, on the other hand, although he was little more capable of forming intimate relationships than was Shaw, needed a sustaining presence, or at least the hope of love. And he clearly demonstrates the collapse into enfeeblement which occurs when grandiose pressure gets a person too much out of touch with reality, and particularly out of empathic contact with people. In his interpretation of Wilde in the novel *The Last Testament of Oscar Wilde*, Peter Ackroyd depicts him in prison being pathetically grateful to anyone who looked on him with kindly eyes, or who spoke words of comfort. Shaw on the other hand had no need for kindly eyes, and he con- tinued to live with strength and energy, at least mental strength and energy, until his death at 94.

Finally, as regards the structural aspect of the self, there is what Kohut referred to as a tension arc between the two poles, which is made up of natural skills and talents. The natural capacities of the child hold the balance between developing ambition at one pole and idealized goals and standards at the other. Kohut used the image of a tension arc to depict this balancing process, and, as the balance is crucial to self-esteem, it is clearly of such importance as to generate a lot of tension. In the end, it is as the achievement of one's ambitions approaches or meets the internal standards that have been set that self-esteem holds, and there is in relation to this balancing process a third, subsidiary type of selfobject experience, one that supports this process and which Kohut referred to as the 'alter ego' selfobject. This is simply the experience of someone being alongside, someone similar to oneself, a peer, a companion, and this is not only supportive but also helpful in mobilizing and using one's talents. It is not using the other as a mirror or as an ideal but simply as a presence to learn with and from. The child learns basic skills and the use of talents by imitation of others, be they parents or siblings or peers, and this process is enhanced and supported by there being a sense of companionship.

A fourth type of selfobject experience has also been suggested. Although it has received less attention, and been less developed, it is worth mentioning as it relates to an important aspect of structure, and that is self-boundary. Adversarial selfobject experience (as it is called) is this further possibility. It relates to the importance in formation of the self of encountering others of different and sometimes opposing views and wishes. It is the experience of the selfobject as a benignly opposing force who continues to be supportive and responsive while allowing or even encouraging one to be active in opposition, thus confirming a developing autonomy. This role is taken as care-takers firmly set limits to what is acceptable in behaviour and what not, while at the same time recognizing the child's contrary wishes, and it is thought that this encounter plays an important part in the child learning what is 'me' and what 'not me'.

Thus, the self-in-action is composed of the essential aspects of the self (true or false, whole or fragmented), the functional aspects of the self in its world of selfobjects (cohesion and strength) and the structural aspect, with its balanced polarity supported by alter ego and adversarial experiences. All aspects work together and all are involved in the developmental process, which is the subject of the next chapter.

Chapter 3

The self in becoming

In the beginning the self has little strength or capacity for self-regulation and acquires these qualities only very gradually throughout the developmental years. Indeed, this process goes on throughout life.

The strength the developmental process brings is in the cohesion and vigour of the self, as well as the extent of its compass (that is, how much of the potential self is actualized). Growth of the self and increase in the capacity for self-regulation come from acquiring the ability to establish and maintain a selfobject state that allows autonomous development and dealings with the world.

Self Psychology sees every human being as having the same propensity for selfhood, although with widely differing skills and talents. The path the development of the self takes depends both on the vicissitudes of selfobject experience and the part that individual capacities play. Significant deficiencies in selfobject experience produce distortions of the natural development of the self. Minor deficiencies, on the other hand, promote development.

Kohut came to recognize the importance of selfobject failure as a result of experience in clinical work. When the people he worked with had established a selfobject transference, when he had become important to the patient in providing particular selfobject needs and he then failed to provide those needs, failed to respond in the desired way, then the patient was likely to suffer a set-back. (The more archaic the needs the greater the intensity of the reaction.) Whether this failure came from an insensitive unawareness, or from misunderstanding of the needs of the patient at the particular time, or simply from being unable to meet the needs, made no difference. The result was the same. The patient lost composure or regressed or symptoms returned; any or all of these were likely to happen, and Kohut came to call such episodes 'empathic failures'. Major failures could disrupt or even derail the process of therapy. In time, however, he also came to see that small failures could not only be satisfactorily resolved but also be used to promote the process of therapy. Once the failure had been acknowledged, and its source understood and satisfactorily explained, then it seemed that the patient gained strength from the experience. It was as if by under-standing the process, people learned to be able to do it for themselves, and a small increment in structure and strength of the self was made every time such an empathic failure was worked through. Kohut called the process 'transmuting internalization'. Once he understood how it worked in therapy, he could then see what a crucial part it played in the developmental process.

Transmuting internalization is a cumbersome term to describe what essentially is a building process. I imagine Kohut used the word trans-mutation to emphasize that it is lasting change that occurs. However, it may be that the choice of word was unfortunate. As I understand it, the result of experience of this sort is more of the nature of adding another brick to the building of the self than it is a change of substance or a conversion. Big transformations can occur but usually the increments are small. Throughout childhood, repeated failures by selfobjects to provide the required experience are used, if they are not too traumatic, to learn to do it for oneself and not to have to rely on others. In this way the child learns not only how to function in the world but also how to be more self-regulating as regards selfobject experience. It is only as mother withdraws from tying shoelaces that the ability to tie laces is learned; and it is only as mother fails to give comfort when a child is hurt that the child learns to be able to self-soothe. Such minor failures are the seedlings of growth. If selfobject needs were always met then self-reliance would never develop.

To see the overall part this plays in the developmental process it is necessary to look in some detail at the growth of a person. Rather than use clinical material for this I am going to use a history taken from a novel, *The Rainbow* by D.H. Lawrence, in which through the character of Ursula, Lawrence attempted to depict the development and achieve-ment of what he referred to as 'the fully consummated self'. The part that empathic failures and resulting transmuting internalization played in her development, as he recounts it, is striking, and an additional advantage of using this material is that her development is set by Lawrence in an historical context of increasing self-realization.

The search for the self is a central and dominating theme in the major works of Lawrence. From the largely autobiographical *Sons and Lovers*, at the end of which the central character 'walks lonelily towards the town, ready and able to be himself despite everything', through *The*

Rainbow and *Women in Love*, in which self-discovery is intimately explored both individually and in relationships, to *Lady Chatterley's Lover*, in which the final attempt to find the ideal self in sexual relationship is made, Lawrence is preoccupied with the meaning and operation of true selfhood. His concern is with the wholeness of being, the full consummation of the self, and for him this is something more than self-assertion, more than cohesion and vigour of the self: it involves a spiritual quality that comes from rootedness in the creative depths of being, and from mankind's peculiar uniqueness.

In *The Rainbow* Lawrence traces the development of increasing self-realization through three generations of the Brangwen family, generations that span the transition from a simple pastoral life to one of increasing industrialization and social complexity.

The Brangwens were farmers who lived in rich farming country 'with heaven and earth teeming around them'. They knew 'the intercourse between heaven and earth, sunshine drawn up into the breast and bowels, rain sucked up in the daytime'. They felt 'the pulse and body of the soil that opened to their furrow for the grain and clung to their feet with a weight that pulled like desire'. Such is the tone of Lawrence's lyrical description of the setting of the novel. He describes the embeddedness of these men in the soil, in a life that had changed little for many generations, and in which there was an inextricable bodily communion of earth and men, all of which he portrayed in a very down-to-earth way using vivid images of sexual encounter.

Such was the solid grounding of these men, but it had limitations. They were so caught up in labour and the soil that they had little awareness of what was happening in the outside world, little appreciation of the changes that were occurring. The women were different. They at least had the time and vision to see the wider scope of life. They were aware of the greater opportunities available to the children of the local vicar, and through the activities of the squire and his wife they could get some impression of the exciting changes that were afoot, and saw the increased opportunities that could be available to their children through education and broader experience.

And it was a time when big changes were starting to occur: the year 1840. The first action described is the building of a canal connecting the newly opened collieries in the area. The canal shuts off the Brangwen farm from the nearby town which is growing rapidly from industrial expansion. The men on the farm are kept busy producing supplies for the town, and they become richer. The farm is on the quiet side of the canal, however, where it remains remote and untouched by the changes.

In placing his novel in this way, Lawrence reminds us of the importance of the non-personal world of selfobjects, of tradition, social stability, a place in the natural order of things, in providing a sense of constancy which gives grounding to the self. In their remoteness the Brangwens were holding on to this: a social context in which all individuals had a permanent place and which gave life a sense of intactness and purpose, and more than that. It provided a vivid and nourishing relation to the cosmos, which for Lawrence is the essence of a religious sense.

This then is the grounding of the self from which the novel starts, and whereas such grounding provides meaning and security it also causes constraint. There is little opportunity to break free from the pre-ordained pattern, and, as change starts to occur, an embankment is required to shelter the settled state of life, and, we may think, the settled state of the self. For most of the people who lived there it provided little opportunity for true individual expression, only an assigned role to fill. For most, the horizon could be extended only vicariously through the privileged few who had access to the wider world.

The parents of the first of the Brangwens who started to break free are described as 'knowing nothing of each other yet living in separate ways from one root', a description that clearly defines both the rootedness and the lack of self-awareness. Their youngest son Tom was his mother's favourite, and she determined that he be sent away from home to a boarding school. He did poorly at the school and suffered great shame and frustration in consequence; after he finished he was glad to get back to the farm 'where the whole place was so kin to him as if it partook of his being'. His selfobject world was still tied to his home and, having found life difficult in the wider world of boarding school, he needed to return home to stabilize himself. Shortly afterwards his father was killed and, the older brothers having moved away, the running of the farm fell to Tom.

He had no difficulty with this but as time went by he became increasingly unsettled. He found nothing in the girls of the neighbourhood to attract him, and he had occasional glimpses of a freer and more cultured existence which disturbed him. He longed for a soul-mate, but could see no prospect of that. We can think that it was hard for him to be content in his enclosed world because he had seen the possibility of a wider world and greater individuality. At home, however, he at least felt safe though lacking in something.

He began drinking a lot. Then he saw a strange woman in the village who immediately attracted him. She was housekeeper at the manse, and he learned that she was the widow of a Polish doctor who had died in London, where they had sought political asylum. Her name was Lydia

Lensky and she had a young child, Anna. Two other children had died when she was in Russia with her husband, working as a nurse. Therefore she was a person of very different life experience and culture from Tom Brangwen's: a woman older in years who had experienced a lot and suffered greatly. Nevertheless, Brangwen was strongly drawn to her and after a few brief meetings resolved to marry her.

Their relationship in marriage was at first uneasy. The gulf between them was great. She was the daughter of a Polish landowner and as steeped in the countryside as Brangwen, but of a higher social class. She told him of life in Poland but he could make no sense of it. Although there were times of intense passion, there were also times when he felt so disturbed by her strangeness that even 'the furniture of the house no longer seemed real' (his selfobject world was under threat). For her part, it irritated her to be so aware of his separateness, and it made her lapse into 'a sort of sombre exclusion'.

Then she became pregnant and bore him a son, after which they came to a confrontation. She challenged him that he wanted more than there was between them, that he wanted another woman who could be more to him. She felt that he came to her as though she was nothing to him. Furthermore, she wanted him to meet her, not bow before her and serve her. At first he held back from the challenge, but then the withholding gradually relaxed in him. He began to move towards her, 'to be with her, to mingle with her, losing himself to find her, to find himself in her'.

In this way Lawrence describes the consolidation of their relationship, thus suggesting that there was a degree of mutuality involved and that Tom had achieved some individuality. *She* took him to her, but not in submission. *He* knew her differentness no better but 'he knew her in a different way, he knew her meaning'. It is clear, however, that this consolidation of their relationship was largely a merger. Referring back to the Brangwen parents who were rooted together in unknowing separateness, we can see that Tom and Lydia had something in common in their roots but in no way approaching sameness. They were not rooted together in terms of selfobjects. They were very different indeed. Tom still lived in the family home which was 'so kin to him that it partook of his being'. He lived predominantly in the world of mirroring selfobjects. In complete contrast, Lydia had long ago left behind her native soil in following her husband in the pursuit of his ideals. When he died, she became a woman alone in the world. Having lost her idealized selfobject she was stranded in abstraction. Tom and Lydia's coming together can be seen as his taking her into his concreteness, or mirror world, and her taking him into her abstraction, or idealized world, and in this way they merged. However, they were both so constrained by their selfobject status that they had little freedom to develop individually, or ability to truly discover the other. Nevertheless, there was some personal differentiation and recognition. He came to know her meaning. She was aware of him as a separate power. They had moved a little beyond unknowing rootedness.

The central characters of the second generation of the novel are Anna, Lydia's daughter, and Will, a Brangwen and a nephew of Tom's. Anna was born in London when her father was near death. For a time she was sole companion and comfort to her mother, who lived through a long period of depression after the death of her husband. When mother married Tom Brangwen, Anna resented his intrusion and clung ambivalently to her mother, partly in the role of protector. Anna's distress was very great when mother was in labour with Brangwen's first child, and it was then that Tom, taking her in his arms to feed the cows in the barn and managing to soothe her great distress, established a close relationship with her. In the description of the inception of this idealizing relationship, a description which is regarded as one of the finest passages in English literature, Lawrence catches in a beautiful way both the calming and the strengthening aspects of the idealized selfobject, which Kohut was later to come to recognize and so clearly define.

After the birth of the baby, Anna felt freer. She no longer had to support her mother and became 'an independent forgetful little soul, living from her own centre'. Later she exploited the idealizing aspect of the relationship with her stepfather by becoming his constant companion around the farm and on trips to the town. When 9 years old she was sent to school, and there she was disconcerting with her indifference to respectability and lack of reverence. She was both shy and wild. She hated people to come too near to her. She had plenty of acquaintances but no friends. Later she was sent to a school in Nottingham where she at first became absorbed in becoming a young lady, but then was disillusioned by the superficiality of it all. We can say she was a strong personality, but one whose firm ground lay in idealizing selfobjects and who had little need for personal closeness.

Will Brangwen came from Nottingham to work near the Brangwen farm. He was a strange youth, dark and rather mysterious, both shy and curiously self-assured. He was interested in churches and church architecture, about which he talked with a 'kindling passion'. He also had a passion for wood carving, and at the time he met Anna he was working on a panel which he called the Creation of Eve. When they became lovers he was resolute for marriage in the face of parental objections to their youth and unpreparedness. After they married he revelled in their intimacy, shut off from the world around.

When Anna insisted on resuming her independent living, however, tension between them began. This tension ultimately resulted in Will destroying the carving he was working on. He could not accept Anna's independence and outwardness. For her part she could not share in his darkness, his spirituality, his immersion in symbolism, his love of churches, his need for a womb. She was too independent a spirit to allow herself immersion in that, and, as we have seen, she had a fear of closeness. Tom and Lydia could form a merger and exist contentedly in that. Will and Anna, having a more developed individuality, could not do so and at times clashed bitterly.

Here Lawrence is presenting the polarity in human nature of light and dark, conscious and unconscious, cerebral and sensual, and the difficulty of reconciliation when there is marked polarity either within a person or within a relationship. In terms of selfobject function, the Brangwen men were still rooted in the immediate and the concrete, still largely in the world of mirroring selfobjects. Although this was spiritualized by Will, by translation into myth and symbol, it was still an experiential womb, a dark enclosure. The women, on the other hand, had moved into brightness, into abstraction, into idealizing selfobjects as the dominant mode. Anna's mirroring had been deficient, as it always is with a depressed mother, but she was able to use Tom Brangwen as an idealized selfobject and achieve a considerable degree of strength and independence thereby. She liked, however, to be out in the open. It was not surprising that she was drawn to someone completely different from herself in this regard, and not surprising too that Anna and Will had difficulty meeting. They had achieved a degree of individuality but lived in different selfobject worlds. They were polarized in separation, and in order to provide for herself the opposite pole to her independence and brightness, Anna moved into the darkness of motherhood and bore many children.

In contrast, in Will there was a darkness that could not unfold. Ursula was the first of their children and 'from the beginning the baby stirred in him a deep, strong emotion he dared scarcely acknowledge'. He wanted the child to perceive him; to acknowledge him; to give him some deeper sense of confirmation; to mirror him. When after a year a second child was born he took Ursula 'for his own'. She became the child of his heart. When she was capable of doing so, nothing would delight her more than running to meet him as he returned from work. In relation to Will, she developed a sense of object constancy. As Lawrence describes it, she came to know her father's coming and going, whereas when mother returned she merely became present with no relation to previous departure. Lawrence also describes Ursula's selfobject relationship to her father precisely in the terms of Self Psychology:

> when he was in the house, the child felt full and warm, rich and like a creature in the sunshine. When he was gone she was vague, forgetful.

When Will became overburdened and irritable, 'her heart followed him persistently in its love', so that she came to know not only a sense of constancy in the relationship but also change of mood, and in this way her father was the dawn in which her consciousness of herself awoke.

As she grew a little older, as well as enjoying his presence, Ursula began to want to help Will when he was doing things around the house, despite this bringing her face-to-face with her smallness and inadequacy. With her father well established in an idealizing selfobject role, she entered on transactions with him which brought significant transmuting internalization. When she tried to help him plant potatoes and he criticized what she did, 'she ran away forlornly to restore herself playing with water, which she loved', and so learned to calm herself through his occasional empathic failures. But then, when playing carelessly in the garden, she trampled on his seed bed. He got in a rage with her, and she in return became sullen and silent, which only made him the more angry. Will threatened to hit her but she remained shut off and apparently indifferent to him. When he was gone she crawled under the parlour sofa to lie and sob for a time 'in the silent, hidden misery of childhood'. In this way, in Lawrence's words, to 'harden her soul, to harden herself upon her own being'. Here is transmuting internalization, and it is from repeated, small interactions of this sort that the self gains strength and composure, and learns to be effective in the world. Lawrence describes the process so clearly that it is necessary to remind ourselves that he is writing fifty years before Self Psychology came into being.

He continues the description of Ursula's special relationship with her father: 'as she got older, 5, 6, 7, the connection with her father was even stronger although always straining to break as she was moving into her own separate world of herself.' Then came episodes in which Will eventually went too far. In warm weather they would go swimming. At first, before she was able to swim, he took her on his back. She was fearless, and later she dared to ride on his back when he jumped from the canal bridge into the river below (and there could be no better image of self-confidence being learned in a selfobject relationship than that). Then, when the fair came to the village, and she went on the swing-boats, she let him push her higher and higher till the people who were watching told him to stop. Afterwards Ursula was violently sick. Will told her not to tell her mother but Anna got to know of the escapade and was very angry with him. When Ursula saw his reaction to this 'a disillusion came over her, her soul became dead towards him and she went over to her mother'. Mother again became the centre of her world and she had less to do with her father. She had returned to the world of mirroring selfobjects as her primary support. It was fortunate she could do so, or the break in the relationship with father could have had a disruptive effect on her development. It could have been a traumatic empathic failure, but was not so. Rather, it helped her development to be more balanced.

So ended a stage in the relationship between Will and Ursula which later on again became very important, but we need not go further with it here. Will at that stage had pushed Ursula too far and caused a major empathic failure. Lawrence's image of the swing-boat is a particularly apt one, and interestingly one that was also used by Kohut, who reported it as a significant dream of one of his patients. He interpreted the dream image as representing the idealizing transference which allows the patient to extend herself and grow, but protects against over-stimulation and going too far into exhibitionism and grandiosity. How amazing it is that Lawrence not only gives a fine, naturalistic account of what Kohut learned from his patient, but used the same image in doing so.

As well as the building of the self that comes from the processes we have been examining, there are also adjustments and adaptations to selfobject failures that cannot be constructively used and result in defects in the self, although they can be compensated for. One pole of the self can compensate for deficiencies in the other, as Shaw was able to compensate for the almost total lack of mirroring in his early years by exploiting idealization as a way of building an extremely stable self structure.

Kohut suggested that the adjustments that are made to selfobject deficiencies are of two types: defensive and compensatory. In *The Restoration of the Self* he writes:

> I call a structure defensive when its sole or predominant function is covering over the primary defect in the self. I call a structure compensatory when, rather than merely covering a defect in the self, it compensates for this defect.

These adjustments bring about a functional rehabilitation of the self, and in the developmental process idealization provides a second chance of forming a cohesive self, of which Shaw is such an outstanding example. With his strength and brilliance of mind he had the ideal talents for such a strategy. For him self-respect came by virtue of work, and work became his mistress. He lived largely in the abstract world of ideas.

As regards defensive structures, these are seen by Kohut as the self-supporting use of the exhibitionist side of the personality, in such forms as extravagant dramatization of behaviour and sexualization of relationships, strategies which are used to hide deep feelings of self-doubt and unworthiness. This type of defensive adjustment is more likely to be necessary when mirroring has been inappropriate rather than simply lacking. In childhood, grandiose fantasies may be used to overcome loneliness (creating an imaginary companion is a common form of this). In adolescence, defensive adjustment may involve intense if fleeting devotion to romanticized aesthetic, religious or political aims. Feelings of inner detachment and depression (symptoms of a deficient self) may be counteracted by an excited hyperactivity which lacks staying power. Such are some of Kohut's specifications of defensive structures, and much of this can be seen in Oscar Wilde. Indeed Kohut's succinct statement that 'intensely exhibitionistic aspects of the personality do not become alloyed with mature productivity' seems to apply to Wilde particularly poignantly.

Compared with Shaw, Wilde was lacking in energy and staying power, and there is every indication that he fell short of fulfilling his great potential as a poet. He is reported as having said that he put his genius into his living and only his talent into his writing. Perhaps it might be more true to say that his energy was too narcissistically engaged to allow the full flowering of his genius.

However, because structures are labelled defensive, it does not necessarily mean that they are less adaptive, and in his extravagant drawing attention to himself Wilde was at least attempting to heal the primary defect. Shaw, on the other hand, adopted a strategy and posture that discounted his emotional and relational needs, yet with this superstructure was able to fulfil his ambitions with remarkable success. It can be argued that Shaw's success was only apparent, that his vigorous and creative living was on a shallow basis, that he was very limited in his ability to form close relationships and that he lacked the personal warmth and charm of Wilde. There is much substance to this, but there remains a striking difference between these two men, particularly in the energy they were able to put into their creative work, despite the fact that there is every reason for thinking that, behind the bravado, Wilde was as passionately committed to being a great writer as was Shaw.

This raises the question of psychic energy, and the part it plays in the developmental process. What is it that determines available psychic energy? What sustains the vitality of the self? We have already seen that mirroring is an immediate energizing factor, as when a speaker is enlivened by an admiring audience. In the longer term, a state of attunement, either as an immediate reflection or as a more sustained and deeper relationship quality, is a crucial factor in the determination of the vitality of the self, and this supplies a satisfactory explanation for Wilde's fall into enfeeblement when he lost his admiring audience and what little empathic relatedness he had.

On the face of it, however, it does not explain the unflagging zeal of Shaw, who certainly liked making a stir but had little need for admiring reflection, and who had few, if any, relationships of a deeply empathic kind. Unless, of course, there are other states of attunement than to persons, other forms of energizing reflection and empathic engagement. For instance, could it be that Shaw was sustained by his vital relationship to literature and music, and, perhaps more importantly, could his energy have been maintained by keeping in touch with his daemon? These questions seem to take us beyond what can be understood psychologically, to take us into the realm of the spirit, but the fact is that psychology of itself has as yet no satisfactory explanation of psychic energy, unless the Freudian view of biological drive as the sole source is accepted.

There is, however, another possible source of Shaw's steady light, one that has already been referred to: that is, the energizing effects of living in touch with one's true self. Could it be that, with Shaw, narcissistic delight in the self could continue unabated because true-self functioning had not been contaminated to any great extent by compliance (he seldom had to do what anyone told him), and grandiosity had not been challenged and compromised by failure to do what he had in him to do? He certainly remained true to himself to the end, and his intellectual powers were truly amazing.

This raises the final issue regarding the developmental process to consider here, and that is the growth of self-esteem. Self Psychology sees the beginnings of self-esteem in a natural delight in self-discovery. Such narcissistic delight is the primary source of good feelings in and about the self, but, as development proceeds, the grandiosity and omnipotence which at first are part of that must submit to the claims of reality. Disillusionment must occur. Moreover, the constraints of what is allowable behaviour, along with the pressure of ideals and values, demand that some control of natural exuberance be established. This particularly applies to sexual exuberance, but to other activities too. Adults find the very active child hard to bear, and, except when the first steps are being taken, there is a cultural tendency to disapprove of anything that smacks of being narcissistic (getting big-headed is one of the least tolerated things in childhood). Children, thus, tend to be subjected to deflationary pressures, and this can have a diminishing effect on hopes and ambitions. At the same time there is, or at least has been, a tendency to set high standards and ideals. With self-esteem being strongly influenced by the extent to which the fruits of ambition measure up to the demands of ideals and standards, there is clearly a problem when a child-rearing process tends to deflate natural spontaneity (the source of ambitions) and at the same time sets high standards. It is a prescription for low or shaky self-esteem, and this may have become a distinct feature of Western society in recent times.

A satisfactory oucome of the developmental process could be seen to result in:

1 Having a cohesive and balanced self in which any defects are effectively covered or compensated for, so that good relationships can be made and maintained.
2 Being sufficiently in tune with true-self needs and having sufficient empathic relationships to provide a good, steady supply of energy.
3 Having stable self-esteem which allows a natural exuberance while meeting good standards of personal and vocational effectiveness.

This may seem to set an ideal, and one that is difficult to attain, but it is a way of looking at child development that allows for failure without it necessarily being pathological. The next chapter will attempt to define this failure in terms of disorder of the self.

Chapter 4

The self in disorder

Throughout the course of life the self is vulnerable to insufficiency or unfittingness of selfobject experience. When these deficiencies are great, and particularly when it is so during the early developmental years, then there may be lasting damage done to the self in its essential, functional or structural manifestations. No arbitrary definition can be made, however, of what is regarded as disorder of the self. All that can be said is that failure to achieve cohesion, vigour or harmony of the self may be regarded as a state of self-disorder if it significantly interferes with competence and enjoyment of living in a lasting way. A simple, descriptive account of some of the ways this can happen is all that will be attempted here.

Whereas damage to the self can be done at any time of life, there are ages and stages when the self is particularly vulnerable. It is so at the earliest stages of development, but also at times of major readjustment, the so-called life crises, such as adolesence, marriage, parenthood, mid-life and retirement. It is at the earliest stages, however, when the vulnerability is greatest, the time, that is, of archaic selfobject need. Then, selfobject function is needed for the very continuity of the self, needed in an absolute and immediate way to avoid psychic death, so that failure of the required selfobject experience at that stage results in unbearable states of dread.

As a consequence, when such unresolved archaic need is later exposed, as can happen in states of regression, it is necessary for the person to create at least the illusion of omnipotent control of the object whose function it is to satisfy the need. At this level, selfobject failure produces profound and very evident effects. It is when such need is brought into the open that therapists may be exposed to the extreme demands of being totally available, all-knowing or unfailingly empathic, and be reacted to with intense disappointment and extreme anger if they fail to be so.

At later developmental stages, when a nuclear sense of self-cohesion has been more-or-less formed, selfobject function is required simply for continuing security and the regulation of self-esteem. Threat to the beginning stage of self-cohesion is less dramatic than threat at the archaic level, is more in the nature of separation anxiety, which is the reaction when absence of the selfobject-caretaker threatens to disintegrate the beginning organization of the self.

These then are the stages at which the most severe damage to the self can be done, and such damage can result in lasting impairment. But it can also happen to a lesser degree and with less severe consequences during later life crises, if selfobject deficiency is severe enough. This is particularly so during adolescence when profound problems of identity may result, or patterns of behaviour be adopted, such as delinquency or drug abuse, which may result in a major failure of the developmental process.

As regards how it happens, disorders and defects of the self can either be due to the direct effect of selfobject failure or be secondary to affective reaction to the failure, and we will examine some aspects of the latter first.

There are three main types of affective reaction. First, there is the effect of selfobject failure as it diminishes the pleasure, pride and efficacy-sense which are the natural accompaniments of good mirroring. Where mirroring is deficient or of low intensity, then the buoyancy of these affects is not available to the self which consequently lacks vigour and vitality. When this has happened over long periods of time the condition of low vitality may become chronic.

The second type of affect disturbance is when there has been a lack of calm holding, necessary for the containment and integration of the painful emotional reactions experienced when the self is being damaged or threatened. This holding is provided by the idealized selfobject. Painful feelings of dread, depression, anxiety, hurt, etc., which are the natural accompaniments of a self under threat, and which the self has not been able to integrate because of the idealizing selfobject failure, can be the source of a lifetime vulnerability to traumatic states.

Of particular significance is the depressive reaction to loss or separation. Reliable and consistent empathic attunement, which helps the child to identify and tolerate this affective state, is necessary to establish the processes of grief and mourning, by which the loss is healed and the self's wholeness restored. A child has to be empathically held to be able to grieve, and when this fails a further loss occurs: the loss of the part of the self that was engaged with the object. Thus, when a parent is lost in early life, a vital part of the self can also be lost, and this kind of loss –

since it is not only loss of a person but any major loss that can have this effect – may be one of the most common causes of defects of the self.

D.H. Lawrence was very aware of such tragic consequences. He felt that people may not only be denied the possibility of a full life as a result, but also lack the courage to face the split-off feelings within themselves. In an essay with the striking title of 'A state of funk' he claimed that some men are at the mercy of feelings they cannot identify, because they did not have the necessary help to integrate them at the time they were first experienced, and therefore they cannot 'realize' them, cannot live them. In particular they are unable to verbalize them, and such inarticulateness has frightful consequences. He writes: 'and so they are tortured. It is like having energy you can't use – it destroys you.' One of Lawrence's great contributions as a writer was finding the words to express emotional states and thus to be able to articulate affect.

The third main type of affective reaction to selfobject failure is narcissistic rage, the origin of which lies in the childhood experience of utter helplessness in the face of a hurting or humiliating selfobject. When selfobject failure has resulted in the persistence of a narcissistic posture that is self-inflating, then any selfobject failure that threatens this is experienced as a humiliation, or, if severe enough, a mortification. The extreme intensity of these affects is what prompts angry and sometimes vicious reactions to being hurt, and it is an awful sensitivity to carry. Such experiences of humiliation are so unbearably painful because the insult threatens the very continuity of the self, and such impairment can result in a person who is subject to explosions of rage in hurtful situations, with usually disastrous consequences to themselves and to others.

Homicidal and suicidal fantasies can occur and may be acted upon, because the intensity of the affect can remove all reason. The furious outbursts can be alarming to others and very damaging to relationships. And, not only does the reaction do nothing to solve the inner condition, it actually intensifies it by reducing self-esteem and increasing sensitivity. In this way sensitivity to narcissistic hurt by rejection or correcion or criticism goes on growing, and the outcome can be a person exquisitely sensitive to any hurt, who tends to harbour resentments and painful memories, and who lives either with a smouldering animosity ever likely to break into rage or with a coldly calculating hostility which can find satisfaction in punishing anyone who offends.

Narcissistic rage is not only an important aspect of self-disorder in its individual manifestations. It can also become integrated into group experience. Kohut suggested that the people of a nation may unite together in narcissistic rage when feeling vulnerable in the face of a threat to the nation's existence or standing. The threatened loss of anything that is crucially important to the cohesion of a group, and which is a common factor in the self-intactness of the individuals of the group, large or small, is likely to unite them in intense reactions which lack all reason and are potentially very destructive. If there is truth in this it helps us to understand the terrible outbursts of destructive nationalism that have occurred in this century (when there has been increasing exposure of the self), as well perhaps as the increase in social violence now occurring.

Finally, as regards the secondary effects of affective reaction to selfobject failure, there is the further possibility that the reactions may result in internal conflict. Where the positive achievements of the self have not only not been adequately mirrored, but have actually been experienced by the selfobject as injurious to them (as when a mother with unresolved narcissistic needs requires the child to be and do what she wants, and that only, and experiences any individual assertion by the child as an attack on her) then such strivings for self-assertion, and the feeling states associated with them, can be a source of enduring conflict and guilt. Such early conditioning results in a state in which any strong sense of self-expression may be felt to be bad or harmful to others. The urge to self-expression is still there, but because of repeated interactions with a damaged selfobject it has come to be feared, and to be a source of guilt. Terrible it is when the joy and satisfaction of 'being oneself' is feared, not only because of the possibility of rejection but also because it is feared that it will actually do harm. As this fear operates below consciousness, the person does not know that it is happening and there-fore can do nothing to change it. Such a state of paralysis of the self is awful indeed, and may be more common than is at present recognized.

A similar process may occur when a child's depressive reaction to selfobject failure is experienced as a threat or as damaging (which is likely with a mother who has had more depression of her own than she could bear and so, to protect herself, rejects her child's depression). When this has been a recurrent experience, the result can be a person who, having part of their self missing, the rejected, depressed part, comes to feel that they are cursed with a fatal flaw, and to perceive others as always likely to be disappointed with them if they show their depressive side.

As an example, Janet first started having periods of depression in adolescence, when she felt an outsider and not like others. She presented for therapy in her twenties after having repeated breakdowns of relationship. As an infant she had spent almost a year in hospital for the correction of a severe congenital deformity which required constant surgical attention. When she went into hospital mother was pregnant, but the child born shortly afterwards survived only a few days. There were also other family losses at the time.

Later in childhood Janet felt very angry because her being in hospital was treated as if it had never happened, and also because everyone was so sorry for mother. Later still, when she got into close relationships she soon started to feel a burden. When anyone got close to her, bad feelings inevitably emerged, or at least that is how she experienced it.

As part of attempting to deal with the problem, and having been helped to recognize that it might stem from that very early experience, she obtained her hospital records, and it was particularly distressing to her to read about herself as she was then and not to be able to make any connection.

It is certainly very understandable that with all her own losses mother was too burdened with depression to be able to take any more and that there was reality in Janet's experience of her own suffering as 'never having happened', it not having been reflected back to her. And we can see from this that there was a part of *her* self which had not been integrated, the absence of which became evident whenever she got really close to someone.

In therapy with such a person, when the underlying depression is brought to the surface, the therapist is likely to be experienced as being painfully disappointed with the patient, who will feel driven to make amends. Or the disappointment may be felt with the therapist who is then criticized. Persistent work over a long period of time may be necessary to break this pattern, but the understanding of what underlies it, and the ability just to stay with the repeated experience of bad feelings happening, gives therapy one of its better opportunities. Provided it is not at too early a level, as possibly it was in Janet's case having been during her first year of life, it is one of the common types of damage to the self amenable to correction.

The direct effects of selfobject failure will now be examined according to how they affect the three aspects of the self: the essential, the functional and the structural.

For the essential self, what matters is the extent to which a child's authentic being is affirmed and strengthened or, otherwise, the extent to which compliance with external constraints contrary to the child's own beingness is imposed. Ideally, it is the total recognition of and response to the uniqueness of the child that results in the promotion of true-self function and produces the full uniqueness of a person. In practice, however, what matters is not the ideal, because that seldom if ever occurs. What matters is that at least there is some choice. To the extent that a child does not have a choice in the selection of what tendencies, behaviours, characteristics and affects it adopts and integrates into the self, to that extent a false-self structure is formed. The self that results from coercion is false. On the other hand, if the child has some choice, if the particular quality or adaptation adopted is an accommodation rather than a coercion, even though the feature is not entirely of the child's own making, then it does not have the qualities and consequences of false-self function. The child has at least had some say.

What are the consequences of false-self function? First of all, the false-self lacks vigour and when under stress can collapse from lack of energy. It is a state of reduced vitality. Secondly, false-self structure needs to be carefully maintained. It has been fashioned to provide pseudo-self-confidence and pseudo-self-esteem, and a lot of time and energy have to be devoted to maintaining these. It is not a natural growth, and does not have a natural vigour. It is like a forced plant which has to be given special care and attention if it is to survive. False-self being is a largely joyless parody of life which requires constant re-charging if it is to have any vitality at all: new goals, new successes, new hobbies, new friends, new stimulation.

We can again use Lawrence to give this a more passionate quality. For him passion was given to life by finding out what was truly desired, by reaching for the fullest responses that relate one to reality, to others and to the authentic self. He saw self-discovery and personal sincerity as the first necessities for any kind of satisfaction or happiness in life. In his own words: 'Living consists in doing what you really, vitally want to do, not what your ego imagines you want to do.' But he added that one of life's most difficult tasks is finding out what that actually is. The spiritual and moral quality enters when he says: 'For me it is better to die than to do something that is utterly a violation to my soul.'

Going on to the functional aspect of the self, the effect of selfobject failure there can be seen in its immediate and its longer-term consequences. As regards the immediate, we have already seen how the presence or absence of mirroring responses influences the current vitality of the self. This is a significant matter for therapists, because they too need minimal mirroring if they are to go on functioning effectively, and it can be a major problem with extremely narcissistic patients who demand total attention for themselves, and are unable to give any acknowledgement to the therapist. As a result, the therapist may become bored or uninterested or drowsy, and while it is necessary that therapists not be dependent on responses from patients for their effectiveness, there is a limit beyond which this can only decline.

Another immediate effect on the self comes from selfobject failure that produces narcissistic hurt. If a certain person is part of one's social network and one finds oneself unaccountably snubbed by them, then this can have a markedly deflating effect, even with strong people. Damage and repair of the damage to the self is part of everyday life and goes on all the time.

As regards the longer-term consequences of selfobject failure for the functional aspect of the self, these can be seen to produce particular states of the self which, because they are enduring, influence personality.

At one extreme is what is called the *under-stimulated self*. Here there has been a prolonged lack of stimulating responsiveness from self-objects, and this state has much in common with the false-self state. Such persons lack vitality, and experience themselves as boring, and they tend to use any form of stimulation to create excitement. In extreme cases desperate efforts may be necessary just to preserve some sense of being alive. In childhood such activities as head-banging, compulsive masturbation and dare-devil behaviour can be used. Later on alcohol, deviant sexuality, risky business adventures, jet-setting, all kinds of frenzied life-styles can play a part in keeping the self from flagging. Indeed, any activity can be transformed into pathological excess by the self's need for stimulation to preserve cohesion and maintain a semblance of being vitally alive, and herein may lie the explanation for the ever-increasing need for stimulation that seems to be so much part of the present cultural climate.

At the other extreme is the *over-stimulated self* where there has been excessive or inappropriate selfobject responsiveness so that fantasies of greatness have not been integrated, and there is in consequence a persistent fear of going overboard in behaviour and in aspirations (the childish fantasies remain active in a split-off state and there is always the unease that they may be acted upon). Because of the unconscious fear of going overboard in behaviour, such people tend to be shy and not have much 'go' about them.

In the *fragmented self*, insufficiency of integrating selfobject responses has resulted in a lack of cohesion, in a self prone to partial fragmentation, which means that sense of identity and of continuity of the self can easily be lost. Such people react to narcissistic injuries with a loss of self-cohesion and self-boundaries, as well as loss of poise and co-ordination. They tend to be anxious, hypochondriacal people who are uncertain of themselves socially and clumsy in behaviour.

Finally, in these self states resulting from the effect of selfobject failure on the functional self, there is the *over-burdened self*. Here there has been a particular failure in the idealizing selfobject responsiveness that holds and calms the distressed or troubled child, and from which the child learns in time to be able to soothe itself. When failure such as this has been severe, the affected individual lives in a chronic state of tension and depressiveness from being unable to be comforted, and cannot but overreact to all painful and troublesome experiences. Lives of persistent misery can be the outcome.

Particular selfobject deficiencies may also result in behavioural tendencies which have an effect on personality make-up. The *mirror-hungry* person is impelled to self-display as a way of maintaining a needed level of attention (as, we think, did Oscar Wilde). The *ideal-hungry* person is constantly seeking a powerful individual, programme or social group to identify with, to provide their sense of strength with a fresh impetus. The *alter-ego hungry* person is forever seeking the confirmation that comes from associating with like-minded people in the pursuit of some goal. The *merger-hungry* have such a shaky self structure that they need to feel themselves to be part of another to have any sense of intactness, and with *contact-shunning* types their intense need for others is exceeded by their great fear of rejection, which conflict is resolved by isolating defences.

These are just some of the patterns of interaction that can colour personality; never present in pure form but often with a dominating and clearly distinguishable influence. And, as lesser tendencies, they are present in everyone, as each person in their individual way seeks to maintain the necessary level of selfobject experience to keep their particular self alive and vital.

As a final feature of how selfobject failure can have an effect on the functional state of the self, we can remind ourselves of Stern's work on affect attunement. The child's affective range and capacity is greatly influenced by care-giver responsiveness. Selective attunement and mis-attunement may not only diminish a child's range of affective experience, but can also actually change it. If, as is thought, affective integration is part of the actual building of the self, then such persistent interactions can only restrict and damage the foundations of the building, and if during the developmental process a child's interpretation of its emotional states is blunted or distorted, then self-doubt can only be great. If you cannot trust your feelings, what can be trusted?

Stern also has something to say about the effect of selfobject failure on self-esteem. According to him, with the operation of selective attunement, and more particularly misattunement, there is the possibility of failure to integrate certain experiences, and if this occurs to a significant extent that will mean not only affects, but actual parts of the self too. Parts of the potential that the self has for development are lost. This results in a divided self, because the split-off parts never lose their potential, and there can be little self-esteem in a divided house.

The genesis of two particular personality disorders probably also begins at this point, the so-called borderline and narcissistic disorders which have received so much attention in recent years. They may *begin* at this particular stage of development, but such profound deviations can only occur if there is chronic, persistent selfobject failure of a severe degree.

Simply to provide some idea of the most severe manifestations of self-disorder, here are the main features of these two types of personality disturbance:

Narcissistic

1 Grandiosity (that is, self-importance or over-valuation of one's uniqueness).
2 Preoccupation with fantasies of success, brilliance or power.
3 Exhibitionism.
4 Over-reaction to criticism or rejection.
5 A sense of entitlement and interpersonal exploitativeness along with lack of empathy.

Borderline

1 Impulsivity and self-damaging behaviour.
2 Intense but unstable relationships.
3 Lack of control of anger.
4 Marked fluctuation of mood state.
5 Chronic feelings of emptiness or boredom.

Another feature of self structure which was described as part of the developmental process must also be mentioned here, and that is the part compensatory and defensive manoeuvres can play in the crystallizing of the bi-polar self.

The self is always having to adapt to loss, both within and without, and having to work at trying to minimize the effect of loss, either by defence or by compensation. It would seem to be that whenever part of the self has not been actualized, when there has been a significant failure to integrate a part or parts of the self, then there is not only an effect on self-esteem as previously suggested, but also an inevitable sense of loss. The depressive affect, which is an inevitable accompaniment of loss, may fail to register. It may be strongly suppressed, or actually present but denied. Clinical experience would say that it is always there, however; that the self cannot accept significant loss of its potential without feeling the loss, and experiencing in some way, conscious or otherwise, a depressive reaction. If the loss is not actually experienced, then the processes of grief and mourning cannot do their healing work, and this is the root of the existential depression that must be dealt with if disorders of the self are to be fully healed.

In addition to reactivating the self, or integrating split-off parts that can be redeemed, grieving and mourning for those that have been lost and cannot be re-connected or re-actualized is an important part of therapy, to which we will turn in the next chapter.

Chapter 5

The self in recovery

In his novel *Beware of Pity*, Stefan Zweig gives a vivid description of the change that came over a young man as the result of an unanticipated emotional experience. It happened to him quite out of the blue. The year was 1913. The person was a young army officer who, until this event, had experienced himself as someone of little consequence going through the routine of life in the way to which he was accustomed, having been raised in a strict, unaffectionate family, and then educated at a military academy. Never had he had an intense emotional experience, and never had he been touched by compassion.

In the Austrian army at the time, military regulations prescribed a code of etiquette and honour that had to be conformed to at all times. Therefore when Toni, the officer involved, caused an emotional scene on an important social occasion he feared he had behaved dishonourably, and afterwards he was deeply troubled by what he had done.

The occasion was a dinner to which he felt very fortunate to have been invited, and at which he became carried away by the splendour of the food and wine, and then by the dancing. In the midst of his excitement, he realized that he had not danced with the host's daughter, and on a sudden impulse sought to do so. With difficulty he found her and pressed his invitation, only to see the frail young woman collapse into tearful agitation. He then realized she was a cripple. In dismay and embarrassment he fled the house.

He returned subsequently to try to make amends, was invited once more to dinner, and this was the occasion which changed him so much. After dinner on this second visit, he spent some time alone with the girl and her companion. The two women greatly enjoyed his stories and good humour, at times laughed exuberantly with him, and this was observed with surprise and appreciation by the girl's father. Zweig has Toni reflect on this experience: 'Usually shy and embarrassed, I now experienced a boldness quite new to me. I made them laugh and laughed with them.' Affect attunement had brought the crippled girl to life in a way that was unusual for her, and Toni had experienced a sense of personal power in being able to have such a beneficial impact.

Later, as he was leaving, the girl's father said how much it meant to him to see his daughter happy, and he stroked Toni's arm in warm appreciation. On his way home the young man felt as if his heart would burst as he realized how much he had been moved by the father's action, and how much pleasure he felt at the power he had found in bringing happiness to people. From this came the resolve:

> from now no more of this torpid existence, this beastly lying about! And so, as I strode more and more rapidly through the soft night, I, a young man suddenly wakened to life, resolved with real fervour that from now on I would change my way of life. I would go less often to the cafe, would give up playing billiards and that wretched tarock, would have done once and for all with all those efforts to kill time.

The experience had had a transforming effect.

This is the sort of awakening of the self that therapy hopes to achieve, although it seldom occurs with such suddenness and many are the obstacles to be overcome for it to happen at all. Yet this incident does demonstrate some of the essential features of therapeutic change. First of all there was an intense emotional experience (in this case in a young man who had been strongly disciplined in self-control, particularly in control of emotions) which opened the door to change. Then the time of enjoyable attunement leading to a feeling of empowerment, to a sense of self-agency in being able to make things happen and do some good, and to feel the stronger for it. Finally, the experience of intense empathic resonance which occurred with the old man and which touched the young one so deeply, bringing a new commitment to life.

Empathy and agency are here the important words, and they are probably the key factors in initiating the therapeutic process. Let us first examine empathy.

Kohut came to see empathy as both an instrument of observation, providing its greatest scientific service in the exploration of complex mental states, and as a mode of relatedness which is most exquisitely active in mother/baby interactions. Empathy is a way of recording impressions, not only by using the ordinary sensory modalities of sight, sound, smell and touch, but also by the use of introspection. It is using introspection as an instrument of observation in order to see more clearly and fully – looking at a tree and not only seeing the visual configuration of the tree but also imaginatively seeing it in its living fullness, with its roots active and sap flowing, seeing whether it is bursting into spring or dying into winter, seeing the particular meaning of the tree for that particular time. Seen as such, empathy can be regarded as a product of informed imagination, a way of comprehending the world that is different from the objective-technical but which does not offend the latter. Empathy uses correctly what is immediately available to the senses, but enlarges and enlivens it by imaginatively adding to the perception all that has been learned from previous experience with such an object. This, ideally, is used to create an impression of the object that is as full and as accurate as it can possibly be. And this is essentially what is meant by empathic awareness of another person.

Empathy, as such, occurs when a mother hears her baby cry, observes the child carefully and then allows what she observes to evoke in her a sense of what the child is experiencing and what the child needs, all the time with attention focused on the child. (Failed empathy is when a mother simply uses her imagination without careful and sustained observation. Then she can only project her own thoughts and fears into her child.) It is empathy of this nature that is the starting point of therapy, as the therapist reaches out empathically to the patient, and it behoves the therapist in doing so to ensure that attention is focused on what the patient presents, so that response is based on clear awareness of the other and not on projection. In addition, however, empathy is an important ingredient of the process that produces therapeutic change.

In Stern's view, and at the intersubjective level, affect attunement is an important part of empathy, and it is an interesting observation, which can frequently be made, that when feeling really in touch with another person there is a tendency to follow their posture and movement. It is as if feeling empathically in touch induces a mirroring response. In therapeutic circles, what is called 'affect tracking' has become one of the 'in' requirements of a therapist: tuning in to, and trying to stay with, in a deliberate way, the changes of affect occurring in the patient. It is, however, not only affect that can be attuned to at the intersubjective level but also 'inner being', which gives the sense of knowing and being known at a deep level, of being 'in-tune' in a personal way, the longing for which is probably universal. When language is able to capture what is quintessential in such experience, then empathy operates at the verbal level, and such times of shared understanding are likely to be high points of successful therapy.

As well as being an initiator of the process of therapy, empathy can also be seen as a goal to which therapy proceeds. Empathic resonance is a two-way process, and the relationship flourishes not only as the therapist becomes more empathically in tune with the patient but also as the patient is more and more able to be empathic in response. Kohut claimed that strengthening of the self occurs particularly when archaic selfobject needs are replaced by empathic resonance, when the one-sided demands of archaic needs can be relinquished so that an experience of mutuality, including the two-sided resonance of empathy, can occur. But more about that later.

From the patient's position, agency is the main initiator of therapy. Self-agency is authentic prompting from within, as distinct from compliance with external demands and expectations. It is self-directedness, and, as we have seen from Stern's work, this is probably much more active, even in the earliest stages of life, than has previously been realized. When people approach therapy it is fundamentally important that the prompting is from within themselves, and that it is not being embarked upon to satisfy other people or for other requirements. Indeed, it is very unlikely that anything can be achieved if that is not so. It is also important that the prompting comes to have as its aim healing, wholeness and growth.

Agency is also power. It is the sense of having some impact on other people, but also of being able to have some influence on or to make changes to oneself that are experienced as being for the good. Agency, both as initiative and as sense of personal power, is the ground of autonomy, and self therapy can be seen essentially as the empowerment of the authentic self.

Agency of the self is therefore at the centre of commitment to this type of therapy, and yet how can agency act, as it were, on itself? Here we need to address the question of being responsible for oneself, because that is so much part of being one's own agent. Without some sense of responsibility, self therapy cannot occur, and there are two ways in which such responsibility can be understood. Clearly, we cannot be held responsible as agents for all that we are, much of which is biologically determined and a great deal of which is the result of early childhood experience over which we had no control, and in which we had very little say. Yet, if we can look objectively, we see that there is a lot of what we now are that we did bring on ourselves, and the slow acceptance of this is an important and sometimes painful part of the process of therapy. It involves seeing when and how we may have chosen the wrong path, and accepting responsibility for it.

In addition to responsibility as agent, however, there is also the responsibility as care-taker of those aspects of ourselves that we did not bring about, and cannot be held responsible for as agent, but which nevertheless are now ours. We can only be healed and grow, and in particular grow in wholeness, when we have taken full possession of ourselves, and this requires both acceptance of responsibility as agent in bringing about what we are, and bearing the regret and remorse that may entail, and of being care-taker for the whole of ourselves. When we are still blaming others for what we have become, when there are parts of ourselves we still disown, the path to wholeness is obstructed. So, as necessary parts of this therapeutic approach, as well as the agency of wanting to be healed and to grow, there is the equally important agency of taking full self-possession.

So great is the importance of agency to the self that change may well start from some sense of power experienced in a relationship (like Toni finding he could make people happy). The sense of having some impact for one's own good is the starting point of empowerment. This impact may be on oneself or on another. In the following example, that of a patient for whom first finding such power seemed particularly significant, it was on another. She was the child of a depressed, alcoholic mother and a detached father, and from an early age she had been sexually violated by a much older man. Having been a victim, and in a powerless position, over a long period of time, she found some power in herself in adolescence in relation to this man. It appeared that the only selfobject experience of any consistency she had received, and that very limited, was from her father, and we can speculate that, in the absence of reliable selfobjects, she used the abusive relationship with her grandfather as a means of keeping something alive in herself (any form of stimulation can be used to this end when selfobjects are deficient). Having had such early experience, during later adolescence there were times when she would expose herself and be sexually provocative to her abuser in situations when he could not respond. This may have simply been a way of teasing him, or it could have been a form of mirroring because probably he did function to some extent as a selfobject, but more likely it was a way of showing that she had some power over him. Reviewed retrospectively, from the vantage point of successful therapy, it was thought by her to have been a significant turning point. It was the first time she felt clear about her own power. It was possibly the first step in ultimate empowerment of her self, and may have contributed to her therapy being particularly successful.

However, no matter what the truth or otherwise of that may be, what is important to recognize is that agency is a vital function of the self and, in therapy that particularly addresses the self, a sense of agency in being able to make things happen is where change starts for the patient.

Whatever may be its particular requirements, however, and notwith-standing that the starting point is different for each participant, therapy is more a matter of 'meeting' than it is of therapist giving and patient receiving, and it may begin to really move when the emerging agency of the patient, by way of experiencing some positive impact on the therapist and being able to evoke from the therapist something of what is required, meets with accurate empathy and acceptance. While, however, that may be the point at which therapeutic change begins, it is maintained by a particular ambience, and especially by the therapist's attitude of respect, acceptance and understanding. The patient's experience is taken seriously. It is believed in, and, in an atmosphere of increasing empathic engagement, shared understanding is sought and worked for.

It is the therapist's task to 'be there' for the patient, and in doing so incidently to meet some of the selfobject needs of the patient. It is not the therapist's job, however, to try deliberately to meet those needs. To do so would be adopting a grandiose provider role the falsity of which the patient would soon come to recognize. Genuineness is absolutely necessary in healing. Contrivance is inimical. The therapist simply tries to accept, understand and explain, and if patients, despite painful dis-appointments along the way, can come to accept and believe in the therapist 'being there' for them, then the process is likely to result in an improved sense of inner strength and well-being. A selfobject bond has been formed.

Therapy of the self is required by a self that is weakened, or has suffered some arrest in development, or has sustained some defect from injury, or, as a result of any or all of these, has adopted a defensive position that further inhibits its development and functioning. The latter inevitably gives rise to resistance to the process of therapy and will be discussed later. When there is no such obstruction to empathic engage-ment, however, all the therapist needs to do is to allow a selfobject relationship to develop, and then attempt to understand and explain when any empathic failures occur. The particular selfobject needs that emerge, be they for mirroring, idealizing or alter-ego experience, will give a clue to the origins of the problem. The work of understanding will clarify the fault, and the self of the patient, strengthened in an immediate way by the therapist's function as an empathic selfobject, can then re-address from a stronger position what has been faulty, or, putting it another way, re-experience archaic constellations with a stronger, more resourceful self.

Were Stefan Zweig's character Toni to seek treatment, it is likely that the symptoms he would present would be feelings of emptiness and boredom. It would be the therapist's task simply to accept the reality of this experience. Not to suggest that he should not be that way, nor to urge him to do something about it or be in any way judgemental, but fully to accept the experience as his present reality, and then try to understand. Pursuing such understanding may mean coming to see that there was little emotional interaction within his family, that his over-burdened mother had little time to enjoy and admire him, that his father was a rather weak man who did not help to hold the tensions and disappointments within the family so that bad feelings were disavowed or ignored, rather than integrated. Add to this the tight discipline of the military academy and there emerges a convincing understanding of the origin of his emotional limitations. If, while all this is emerging, an empathic bond is established with the therapist, then Toni may be able to start to contact the suppressed affects associated with his deprivations (likely to be rage and shame at what was lacking in his family), and the foundations of the false-self structure he had adopted would be shaken. As he experiences the therapist as a strongly supportive presence, who can help him to bear his pain and who reflects back to him a picture of his inner world, then the changes that Toni experienced in the novel as occurring suddenly can start to come about gradually. In this process it is an idealizing, 'father' transference that would be likely to occur, and which would tune the therapist in to how to respond. While exercising himself to make changes at the outset would have been unlikely to have succeeded, now that some inner change has occurred it would be neces-sary for Toni to exercise himself in new directions if the change is to be developed. In particular, he would need to exercise himself in estab-lishing closer and more emotionally charged relationships, if he is not to sink back into the pre-therapy torpor. The newly awakened self needs exercise if it is to find increased strength, just as does the body after disuse due to injury or illness.

The slow, steady progress which this suggests could have occurred with Toni would be unusual in actual therapy, particularly so when there have been deep-seated faults in selfobject function, and even more so when these have been at an archaic level. The uncovering of such basic faults is likely to have a very disturbing and disruptive effect, and to put a strain on the therapeutic relationship. When a sector of the self is opened up involving suppressed archaic needs, the demands unleashed are likely to be particularly intense and insistent. Such uncovering is a necessary first step in therapy, and becomes possible as the bond between therapist and patient is established, and deeper understanding is sought. The patient starts to feel securely held and safe enough to expose the damaged sector. As the affect associated with the injured self is contacted, then the damaged sector is uncovered; when the injury is deep the completion of the uncovering process can result in an intense reaction in the patient which can be likened to a diver coming to the surface gasping for air. The exposed self-sector is so fragile it cries out for comfort and support, and this can develop quite rapidly. These archaic needs become focused on the therapist and, as there is no possibility of being able to satisfy them at all fully, the patient once more faces the inevitability of being failed and rejected. The demands may be for constant availability or perfect mirroring, complete accuracy in empathic understanding or omniscience and omnipotence, but whatever their particular nature they are absolute. There can be no negotiation, and no matter how astute and careful the therapist is, painful disappointment and disillusionment are bound to occur. Then the patient is likely to collapse into fearful turmoil and rageful criticism at having once more been thwarted and deeply hurt, and then the work of repair begins, starting with acceptance.

Such traumatic transference reactions occur when there has been deep damage to the self, but they are also characteristic of people who have been exposed to extreme physical threat and violence, as documented and so well described by Herman in her recent book *Trauma and Recovery*. When there has been great trauma, including sexual trauma, the experience of terror has so deformed the victim's emotional reactions to people in authority that explosive reactions are likely to occur in response to any failure on the part of the therapist. The fear of this happening can result in intensely idealized expectations, and the need to control the therapist. But when this fails, hurt and rage erupt. Herman writes about this:

> when the therapist fails to live up to these expectations – as she inevitably will fail – the patient is often overcome with fury. Because the patient feels as though her life depends on her rescuer, she cannot afford to be tolerant; there is no room for human error.

Such is the reality of traumatic transference reactions, and such is the nature of archaic selfobject transferences.

If an empathic break of this intensity is to be repaired it is incumbent upon the therapist to accept the patient's reaction, no matter how unreasonable it may be. It is simply accepted as happening, and not questioned as to whether or not it is justified. Then with tact, and empathic understanding of the distress of the patient, and the shame likely to be felt about how they are behaving, the therapist carefully encourages exploration of the cause of the breakdown – what the crucial disappointment was and where the roots of such sensitivity may lie. It is a process that requires courage on both sides, but, as the exploration becomes a shared task, then patients come to feel that they have had some impact which has produced a helpful response: a sense of agency is confirmed. With agency can come the mutuality of negotiation, because negotiation can only come from strength, and as this creates a shared understanding, a reciprocal empathic flow is restored and in the process the structure of the self is strengthened. Acceptance through negotiation to mutual understanding is the path, and the immediate destination is the restoring of the empathic bond. Acceptance by the therapist includes accepting having been a failure at the time of disjunction, not in any guilty, self-condemning way but simply that it was a real part of the interaction.

It is understanding the archaic roots of the patient's demands that helps the therapist to accept and not condemn. The crucial experience for the patient is the sense of agency in having some impact on the selfobject world which produces not rejection but a holding and confirming response. It is this sense of agency which, gradually growing through helpful responses to repeated empathic failures, eventually results in growth of self-confidence in being able to maintain one's own selfobject world, and not be so dependent on others. It is this confidence which brings freedom from the archaic selfobject world where dependency is absolute, and gives the strength to embark on interpersonal negotiations that bring freedom from addictive-type relationships.

It is working through many such empathic failures that gradually strengthens the defective area of the self, or for the first time gives the self some firm structure. The latter is what happened over two years of intermittent therapy with the sexually abused patient who was previously mentioned, and it is amazing indeed that such profound deficiency and severe damage can be corrected, at least to some extent. But such surprising changes do at times occur, even for the severely impoverished or damaged self.

A further consequence of repeated disruption and restoration of the therapeutic bond is that the patient comes to sense and appreciate empathically the therapist's acceptance and commitment to understanding, which can then become mutual. In this way empathic resonance grows, and the vicious cycle of faulty selfobject response causing further fragmentation and leading to more faulty responses is replaced by a cycle of right responsiveness leading to greater strength and cohesion, and to better functioning. Interactions that bring the worst out of the participants are changed for ones that bring out the best.

Whereas therapy of the self is in this way a natural process that gathers its own momentum once it gets under way, sometimes getting the process started can present enormous difficulties. At the severest degree of damage, a weakened self is in danger, if it is opened up, of regressing to total fragmentation, to what amounts to dissolution and death of the self, to a sense of annihilation, and the intense dread this generates prompts the establishment and maintenance of defences that do not allow the uncovering of such a weakness. Any attempt to challenge or understand such defence is likely to be resisted strongly, and can be experienced by the patient not only as a threat but also an intrusion, even a persecution.

In addition to the weakness of the self being a source of resolute defence, there are two other fears that can cover and block the emergence of archaic selfobject needs: the fear of losing all autonomy and independence and the fear of being exposed again to terrible hurt. All a therapist can do when resistance is strong is to maintain an accepting and empathic stance, and to seek to understand and explain. The fears of exposure are talked about, and the dread of total collapse recognized. The patient will tend to deny any inner fault and to keep the problems on the outside. The therapist must direct attention to the inner world. There, despite denial, there is likely to be a glimmer of the self's true needs, or otherwise the person would not be seeking therapy, and it is when this tiny hope establishes connection with the empathic responsiveness of the therapist that the first step in reducing resistance is made.

When this happens, a further obstacle emerges as the patient starts to sense the clamant nature of the archaic selfobject needs, bringing with it the threat of the shame of such extreme dependency and such unreasonable demands. Despite this, however, empathic responsiveness, acceptance and explanation can now start to be more actively engaged, until such time as a selfobject transference is established and the natural process of healing can begin.

During this preliminary period, the therapist acts mainly as an idealized selfobject who is able to hold and contain and understand the disturbing emotions that are stirred. Affects are of great importance as signals of self-distress, but they cannot be used when they are too intense or chaotic because they threaten the very existence of the self. When, however, they are recognized and responded to, as it is the therapist's task so to do, then the fear of loss of continuity of the self is lessened. With the therapist's sustained holding, and the reduction of fear, the chaotic nature of these affective disturbances subsides and the patient starts to be able to use them as self-signals. The inner world starts

to make some sense, and the belief that affective needs are not acceptable, and may even be shameful, gradually loses its grip. Defences can
then be lowered and the natural process of therapeutic change get under
way. During this process the core conviction of essential badness, which
accompanies all repressed archaic selfobject needs, is laid bare, and at
this point words are of no avail. No understanding or explanation can
correct this depressive core, only acceptance. It is the sincere conviction
of the therapist that the patient is not essentially bad, but *is* essentially
human, that in the end frees.

Therapy of the self, therefore, is a meeting in which occurs the
gradual establishment of mutuality and empathic reciprocity. It creates
an ambience in which the discrepancies of different subjectivities can
become discernible, explainable and understandable. Two different
people meet. The essential consequences of psychological trauma, in a
personal sense, are disempowerment and disconnection from others, and
it is therapy's task to change these. Above and beyond all technicality,
such therapy is a healing relationship between two people.

Self Psychological understanding attempts to discern as clearly as
possible the inner world of another person, and the extent to which the
person is succeeding or failing in finding expression of their true self.
Therapeutic dialogue begins by accepting and addressing the immediate
experience of the other. It seeks, however, to go beyond what is immediate, by helping the patient to come to a true recognition of the state of
his or her self, and on that basis to start to clarify what for them is the
truth of their existence. The self that is free and strong knows what it
wants and how to get it. In the encounter with the therapist the patient
comes to this self-realization.

Seen in this way therapy is, in its fulfilment, a dialogical encounter,
and in the next chapter we will see how this can be promoted instru-
mentally, as well as how it can provide a bridge into the world of the
spirit.

Chapter 6

The bridge

In essence, therapy of the self is the meeting of two selves in the pursuit of authentic being. Of those undergoing therapy it requires a yearning for authentic being and for wholeness. Not that this is necessary from the outset, nor does it necessarily have to be explicitly stated, but self-discovery and personal sincerity must eventually become implicit primary goals if self therapy is to be successful. As part of the process, patients come to accept agency and authorship of their own being, as far as they are able to do so, and to accept the givens of life in the spirit of wanting to make the best of them.

Self-discovery is necessary to provide the enduring sense of personal identity, the established state of inner constancy that is the vital ground of a centred, purposeful and fulfilling life. Without it life can only be a wandering in happenstance. In his autobiography *The Buried Day* C. Day Lewis writes of the problem he had with such sense of identity following the death of his mother, when he was 4. He writes:

> a child first begins to get its bearings and realise its identity by seeing itself reflected from two opposite sides – from its father and its mother: if one of these mirrors is taken away, the child may suffer from bewilderment or from a growing obsession with the question 'Who am I'. Certainly, as a boy, I was often staring into looking glasses, and still do.

Throughout childhood he spent long summer holidays in Ireland with his mother's sisters and brother. These were times of slow routine, of great sensual pleasure and of safe constancy which gave him great delight. To those wonderful times he felt he owed not only the capacity for relishing the everyday, and for recognizing the attractions in the commonplace, but also for a fund of inner calm, 'a sense, even when I am out of my depth, lost and struggling desperately, that there is firm ground not far away'. The firm ground is the self in its context of selfobjects, which that early experience in Ireland helped to create for the young poet, despite his great loss.

There is probably more to self-discovery than that, however. The life of the self provides, in addition to identity and inner constancy, a sense of satisfaction, a feeling of achievement in doing what one has in one to do. This is something Lawrence wrote about with great passion. Real satisfaction in life's achievements comes not from doing better than others but from living to one's own potential, being fully oneself, and this is something that is available to everyone no matter what their assets and talents. Lawrence writes: 'one man isn't any better than another, not because they are equal, but that they are intrinsically other, that there is no term of comparison.' So that, whereas being self-satisfied has tended to be seen as a fault, finding satisfaction in the self may in fact be one of life's most enriching motivations.

Not only, however, did Lawrence write about self-consummation in a passionate way, he also regarded it as a passionate process, giving to life thrill as well as satisfaction. For him self-discovery is no intellectual pursuit but one that involves one's whole being; it is in one's blood, and it brings not only vitality and passion but also at times makes life thrilling. Nothing is more important in life, but also nothing more difficult to find. In *Phoenix 11* he writes:

> Living consists in doing what you really vitally want to do; what the life in you wants to do, not what your ego imagines you want to do. And to find *how* the life in you wants to be lived, and to live it, is terribly difficult.

Such an important and difficult discovery is a part of what the process of therapy is about, and a developing sense of agency in the pursuit of that is a fundamental requirement of the patient.

Of the therapist, the process of therapy requires a clear understanding of the developmental unfolding of the self in a technical way, as well as a good grasp of the manifold obstacles to authentic being, and the ways in which such obstacles can be removed or circumvented. Without these a therapist cannot be an effective guardian and guide. With them, however, empathy can do its work in bringing the self into focus.

At the beginning, empathy can only be with the life experience of the patient as her or his story is told, as well as with the wishes and feelings that are disclosed in the process. As time goes by, however, empathic awareness extends more and more to yearnings for authenticity and wholeness, for the patient's wish to be her or his own person as fully as circumstances will allow.

Having clearly reached this point in her therapy a patient had a significant dream. She reported the dream in the context of talking about the excitement she was finding in self-discovery, but also the difficulties she was having in finding opportunities to practise her new-found 'being herself'. The first act in the dream was of her being raped by a group of men (she had been subjected to sexual abuse in childhood). What was surprising to her was that the experience was not particularly unpleasant, and afterwards she experienced herself as something of a hero for having come through it so well. What did trouble her in the dream, however, was that subsequent to the rape she used the recounting of the experience as a means of gaining sympathy and attention. She felt that this was warped (her word) and she felt embarrassed about it. In recounting this she then went on to talk about how the dream related to herself and her ways of gaining attention, of the levels that fantasy can go to to get attention. To her the dream represented the devious and delinquent ways she had used to get attention. Her ways had been warped. She said, 'If you can get what you want you don't need the garbage', and her longing now was not just for any attention, but for attention she did not have to coerce, or contrive, or submit to, or to bring about by delinquent means. She wanted to forget about the garbage.

There was, however, another important factor in the situation that related to the dream. The sessions were being sound-recorded and it emerged that, as well as the group rape representing her distorted ways of gaining attention, it also represented the group of people who listened to the tape. The microphone was the painless intruder that did not bother her unduly, the painless rape. In this way the dream raised the question as to whether the recording was warping the process. This patient was bringing home to the therapist the importance of the place she had reached. The true self coming into focus is a place for complete naturalness and sincerity, which any pretence or contrivance can only spoil, and the microphone was probably doing just that.

When such a place has been reached, there is then the possibility of a further extension of the empathic process. When there is a mutual sense that the process engaged in is both a commitment to and an experience of self-discovery, and when the authentic self is acknowledged to be present, unprotected and unadorned, then empathic resonance can do its consolidating work. Then the true self is truly strengthened. Then there can be full mutual acknowledgement, which Buber refers to as a dialogical encounter. At this point termination is not far away, because therapy is simply a means of getting self-discovery and self-affirmation started, and when this is well established then it can continue from its own momentum.

Emma was a patient who had been having a very long and difficult struggle to find out how the life in her wanted to live, and to live it. Having grown up in a home where love was not evident, but where there was the expectation and potential for high creativity and academic achievement, she got pregnant in her first bid for freedom, and submitted herself to an abortion. Afterwards, with parental encouragement, she found acceptance and rehabilitation in a fundamentalist religious community. She then married, and this proved for her as lacking in love as her home of origin had been. Children provided her with some warmth, and something to give herself to, but when they were well established at school she decided to leave her husband and begin a professional career, at which she was soon very successful. Despite the success of this, the coldness of her life continued, and, out of increasing sense of self-despair and guilt, severe depression supervened.

Emma had a difficult struggle in therapy, not only because of her deep conviction of unworthiness and unlovableness, but also out of fear. The fear related particularly to the community she joined following her abortion. She had come to feel that there she had been emotionally coerced into something that was not her, and she feared that therapy would be a similar coercive process, the last thing she wanted. Nevertheless she persisted in coming, and eventually her depression started to lift. Following a session in which she addressed the question of what she should call me, not up to then having called me anything, she made an open acknowledgement that she was now quite confident about the process. She spoke of my skill in being a mirror to her. She said that I gave her the space she needed for herself and then reflected it back to her in a careful and convincing way. For my part, I had come to see her as a person of some quality, someone who had the courage to go her own way but who had retained a warm concern; a woman who had taken a feminist path but without hardness of heart; a potentially beautiful woman. In other words my reflection had a lot to give her, and when she gave to me the ackowledgement of what I had been doing for her there was, during a poignant period of silence, a strong empathic resonance between us. It was a very special moment. Later she went on to tell how pleased she had been seeing her son the previous weekend and seeing him at times being very considerate of his father. I saw, and was touched by seeing, how her face lit up warmly talking about this and, when I reflected this to her, tears started to flow and there was an experience of genuine emotional intimacy, of strong affect attunement. Both in terms of empathic engagement and affective contact we were at that special place where there can be no dissembling or contrivance, where a true meeting of souls occurs, and this special place is at the heart of this type of therapy.

With this understood to be the heart of the process, and the importance of agency and empathy in initiating the therapeutic process having been emphasized, we will now give attention to two particular dimensions of the interaction. The purpose of doing this is twofold: first of all, to provide the means of creating a mental and operational frame in which the process can be seen to occur, and understood to occur; and, secondly, to help to build a bridge into the realm of the spirit so that poets and writers can then be used to enlarge and enrich the view.

Before doing this, however, let us first briefly review the understanding we have already come to about the process of therapy. We have seen that therapy of the self truly begins when agency towards healing and growth meets a truly empathic response, allied to an attitude of acceptance, respect and understanding; that in 'being there' for the patient in this way, a selfobject transference from the deprived or weakened sector of the self is established with the therapist; and that, either by the sustained holding of the therapist or by repeatedly working through empathic failures, the defective aspect of the self is strengthened, resulting in greater cohesion of the whole. We have also seen that in the process the relationship moves towards increasing reciprocity in terms of affect attunement and empathic resonance, which are significant sources of cohesion and strength of the self.

To that we will now add reciprocity in terms of power, and, in doing so, instate empowerment as one of the fundamentally important gains of therapy. To this end, I am going to use a model that has been developed to understand the growth of autonomy in childhood, and also give some definition to the instrumental aspects of the exercise of power. The first of these instrumental dimensions is the polarity of initiative and control as exercised in the relationship.

Taking initiatives in and exercising some control over personal interactions are basic features of agency, and they are also grounds for the exercise of autonomy and power. On the basis of developmental studies, Wertheim proposed a model for the development of autonomy in childhood which centres on the exercise of initiative and control. In essence, the model states that the equilibrium of the interactional system between mother and child is constantly being disturbed as the child develops greater capacity for self-generated behaviour. Restoring equilibrium requires that the child's increasing capacity for independent action be matched by mother's acknowledgement and approval, and that new agreements regarding permitted initiative and control, which realistically reflect the child's capacity, be repeatedly reached. Such a gradual process can be seen to occur in therapy, and when it is encouraged by management which allows the patient to assume appropriate control by negotiation, then autonomy is promoted and consolidated, and reciprocity, in terms of power, is increased.

In therapy, although a degree of power reciprocity can be present from the outset, it must necessarily at first be limited, both because of the particular nature of the situation and the fact that mutuality takes time to develop. Even when therapists have an open manner and non-directive approach, the meeting occurs on their ground and conforms to their rules. Moreover, it is only as a therapist can exercise some directive control over the material presented that the information necessary for a competent assessment can be gathered. In the initial stages therefore there is limited mutuality, and it is the therapist who largely determines how the transaction is conducted, and who is in the position of power.

Thus therapy begins from an asymmetrical position, and this can provide a clear directional conceptualization for the process of one aspect of the relationship. The direction is simply from asymmetry to symmetry. In interactional terms, the movement is towards greater equality and dialogue, and explicitly to more power sharing, with the development of the relationship over time being guided by the wish to establish, at least to some degree, a truly personal reciprocity when termination is reached. To achieve this the therapist must not only be willing to let it happen, but must also assist the patient to move in that direction.

The other question, that of how control of the interaction is exercised in a therapeutic transaction, is an exceedingly complex one which cannot be gone into fully here. Some limited specification only will be attempted, using a distinction between the microsphere and macrosphere of the interaction, and how control is exercised in each.

The microsphere is the area of immediate contact and includes the communication strategies and attitudes employed by both participants to exercise control of what is happening between them. Each bit of communication, each transaction on a particular topic or theme, is initiated by one of the dyad, and the direction it takes is determined by one or other as the balance of directive control in the particular episode is established. The minutiae of this interactional issue are too detailed to monitor, and to attempt to do so would obstruct any freedom of response, yet it is always possible, when appropriate, for the therapist to stand back and ask the questions 'Who initiated this theme or topic?' and 'Who is largely controlling the way it is developing?'. Likewise a particular session can be judged by detailing the significant issues taken, and who took them, and allocating the main locus of control during the session. In this way some monitoring of the immediate instrumentality of the interaction as regards initiative and control strategies is possible. With careful attention and practice, it can be done effectively without affecting the flow of the interaction. Such monitoring allows some awareness of the exercise of power in the relationship, which adds a lot to assessment of how the relationship is developing, and where it needs to go.

It must be acknowledged, however, that how an individual expresses initiative and effects control is a very variable and complex matter. Furthermore, people who are in need of treatment are often poor communicators, and are lacking the self-confidence to relate effectively, so that they tend to employ indirect and obscure strategies. At times, for instance, it may be difficult to distinguish true initiative from a persistent introduction of subjects that is simply defensive, and control will frequently be attempted in a passive rather than an active way. Thus a lot of skill is required to decipher communication strategies and recognize the reality of the interaction. These, however, are precisely the skills of an experienced therapist, and if attention is focused on these issues in the immediate transaction, then there can be some awareness of the pattern.

The macrosphere of the instrumental dimension of initiative and control is the overall pattern of control that is established as the relationship develops and comes to termination. Here the intuitive sense of the quality of the interaction is of greatest importance. An experienced therapist can sense when the relationship is moving towards a genuine mutuality, in which control is settled by negotiation between two equals. As a guide, Buber has described the particular qualities of this in considerable detail. Some therapists may use the definition of ego states as a means of appraisal, and chart the development and state of the relationship according to whether 'child', 'parent' or 'adult' ego states predominate. Always there is the possibility of recourse to the immediate instrumentality of the interaction as a way of confirming or disconfirming the assumptions that have been made and are operating. It is as attention is given both to the overall quality of the relationship and to immediate contact strategies, with the one appraisal a check on the other, that confidence in monitoring this aspect of relating is gained. Such confidence gives the therapist the technical ability to move the relationship in the direction of greater mutuality, which is so important when termination is near.

The second instrumental dimension to be specified lies within the therapist. It is the polarity of empathic engagement (participation) on the one hand and objective detachment (separation) on the other, as experienced by the therapist in relation to the patient. Participation at first finds expression in a sustained professional interest in and attention to what the patient says and does, interest which seeks clinical and personal understanding. At times, such empathic engagement may momentarily move beyond attention to what the patient is saying and experiencing to actual identification. In imaginatively experiencing what the other relates, the therapist moves to an extreme of participation, and at such times self boundaries may be lost; merging briefly occurs.

At the separation end of this dimension, self boundaries are clear and self-awareness is the experiential reality. Such self-definition has a reflective aspect, in an attitude of detached contemplation that objectifies self and other, but is most clearly expressed in communications to the patient in which the therapist offers a separate viewpoint. It is when the therapist gives opinions or views that are different from and may be opposed to those of the patient that separation is expressed most emphatically.

This then is the dimension of the experiential state of the therapist between the poles of participation and separation, both of which are essential to any therapeutic endeavour. Without empathic participation, no genuine understanding of the patient's suffering can be realized. Without effective separation, no clear assessment can be made and no personal response offered.

In the microsphere of immediate contact the rapid fluctuation of such experiential states must defy accurate monitoring. Nevertheless, good therapists must always be aware of where they are in relation to the patient, and recognition of these states, and awareness of the dominant mode at any stage of therapy, can not only be an aid to this but also allow a better appraisal of the ongoing process of the interaction. Such appraisal can be an important guide to how therapy is proceeding.

A therapeutic relationship cannot be sustained in the absence of at least the potential for both participation and separation. Participation with the loss of the capacity to separate means that the therapist has lost the ability to be clear about what is self and what is other, what is projection and what is reality. On the other hand, when there is loss of empathic contact which cannot be restored, the relationship, as therapy, has ended.

Sometimes therapists are pushed to an extreme position on this dimension because of the nature of the patient's condition. When a paranoid patient is overwhelmed by persecutory anxiety, therapists will be kept at a distance from which they can only struggle to make empathic contact, often at the time to little avail. At the other extreme is the helpless, depressive patient whose neediness engulfs the empathy of the therapist. When pushed to these extremes, therapists can only acknowledge their position and bide their time, knowing that it is only when both separation and participation are possible, and the dynamic equilibrium between them can be worked on, that progress in the relationship aspect of therapy can be made.

In the macrosphere of the interaction a clear overall pattern is present. Effective therapy begins only when participation is established, and therapy ends with the separation of termination. Within these bounds there is constant fluctuation as the patient's needs move from one pole to the other. Effective therapists must have the flexibility to modulate their stance in response to immediate needs, so that an empathic response is given when needed or separation offered when appropriate. Such right responsiveness is a crucial skill of the good therapist.

If increasing mutuality is to be the goal of the relationship, however, as it moves towards termination, separation must become the dominant mode. Personal reciprocity can only exist between two differentiated selves and such differentiation requires that transference is transcended, and it is here that attention to instrumentality is so helpful and important. An understanding of the vagaries and pervasiveness of transference is necessary, and transference clarification or interpretation may be required, but the experiential recognition of the separation mode, which potential is always present except in the face of severe pathology, allows the therapist to promote differentiation and encourage its further development. Patients can be invited to recognize the importance of speaking from their own individual reality and also to negotiate about control and point of view, and in this way a deliberate move away from transference can be made. An important part of doing this is sensing when the time is right to fix a termination date, and making sure that this is dealt with by open negotiation. In no situation is mutuality in the exercise of power more important. And there can be no better celebration of the resolution of the issue of power than a good ending.

In brief therapies there is always a degree of arbitrariness about termination because it is seldom clear that all work is completed, and incidental factors having nothing to do with therapy often determine an ending. What is important is that termination is anticipated so that the issues of separation and ending can be worked on. A sense of the quality of the relationship, an awareness in its ongoing life of the degree of mutuality that exists, can be an important guide to choosing the right time, in addition to the completion of whatever treatment goals may have been set.

Working on the conflicts of separation is an important part of termination. Such conflicts are frequently present because debilitating affective constellations relating to separation and loss are common components of psychopathology, and are likely to be awakened as termination approaches. A stable, reality-based mutuality, resulting from attention to the instrumentality of the interaction, is the basis from which such conflicts can be addressed in order to come to a good ending. A degree of temporary regression can be allowed, with the therapist empathically engaged in the struggle the patient is having, and being sensitive to the pain involved, but not regression that will threaten the ability to separate.

It is at this time that both participation and separation operate in an intense way, as the therapist senses the pain that separation and loss present to the patient, and the sorrow of parting becomes a reality for both. Much important psychotherapeutic work is done at this time as mutuality grows into a poignant personal reciprocity.

These instrumental dimensions have been introduced into this account partly as a means of creating a cognitive frame for containing the process. A frame requires closure, and it is in the termination phase that these instruments can work synergistically to create a satisfactory ending. We have been looking at some of the significance of participation–separation at termination, but the other dimension is equally important, and the one can potentiate the other.

As the patient increasingly takes initiatives and assumes direct control of the interaction, when it is appropriate, a process which is not only sanctioned but also modelled by the therapist, then differentiation in the relationship is fostered. Each relates more autonomously. The initiative to terminate may come from the patient or from the therapist, but when a decision is reached by negotiation and mutual agreement, then differentiation and personal reciprocity become real and significant.

Thus the two dimensions help to define an end point, and help to build a relationship bridge from which the negativities of ending can be dealt with and a true parting made. Such a termination, in which there is a realistic appraisal and shared recognition of what has been achieved, and of what the relationship has come to mean, consolidates the gains that have been made and allows expression of affect on a personal level which helps to create a good ending. Hopefully this means that the patient can accept the ending, and endure the separation without losing any of the gains that have been made.

Not only, however, do the instrumental dimensions help to create a relationship bridge that is useful at termination, they also help to build a bridge into the world of the spirit. They are signposts not only to reciprocal interaction but, when the self is fully engaged, when each is present to the other with the whole of their being, they lead to what Buber refers to as dialogical encounter, and at this point, so he claims, one enters the world of the spirit.

At such a time each speaks from the truth of their self, moments of which may occur throughout the therapeutic process. When, however, this has become mutually acknowledged as an established mode, not always present but ever there to be regained, then the relationship has taken on a new dimension. A spiritual dimension. It was such a moment that occurred with Emma.

This way of construing the process of therapy receives support from some quite recent developments in Self Psychology. In the context of proposing 'playspace' as a metaphor for the space in which therapy occurs – to quote: 'the place in which is generated experiences which become the core of what we mean by personal selves' – Meares has described two contrasting forms of transference which have some equivalence to what has been meant here by the modes of participation and separation. One form of transference is when the therapist is experienced by the patient as a selfobject presence holding the space and allowing free play to occur, play meaning here an 'associative, feeling-laden, non-linear psychic life, a state of being with another in which those experiences which generate the core self can be created'. This is more a state of communion than of active engagement, and it is like the mother in reciprocal attunement with her baby. The therapist in this mode is not salient but more a background presence providing a holding 'atmosphere'. This is equivalent to the mode of participation. The other form of transference occurs when there has been a disruption of the selfobject transference as a result of empathic failure by the therapist, or for other reasons. In this state the therapist comes to the forefront as an object; becomes an object who can represent different aspects of the patient's experience with frustrating and frightening and disruptive objects. The therapist becomes a 'you', and as such may be made a focus of past conflicts and losses. This is the mode of separation, and it is what has been commonly understood by transference.

Meares suggests that there is constant movement in and out of these different transference states during therapy, and he sees the strengthening of the self occurring as the selfobject state of being together is retained, and as it is re-established after periods of disruption. He does not mention, however, another possibility in the disrupted state, and that is the meeting of two differentiated selves. Disruption may not only be the breaking of the empathic selfobject bond, with the emergence of 'it' relatednes, but it can also provide an opportunity for the empathic relating of dialogical encounter, an I–Thou relationship, which is what we will explore more fully in the next chapter where we move into the realm of the spirit.

Chapter 7

The spirit in essence

Radhakrishnan describes the life and fruits of the spirit as:

> To know, possess, and be the spirit in this physical frame; to convert an obscure plodding mentality into clear spiritual illumination; to build peace and self-existent freedom in the stress of emotional satisfactions and sufferings; to discover and realise the life divine in a body subject to sickness and death.

In this view, 'being in the spirit' is in essence an independent and clear functioning of the human mind: the psyche freely and fully engaged in life; a mind functioning in its uniqueness as it relates to a reality untainted by preconception or by distortion. And to this emphasis on the freedom of the functional aspect of the mind Radhakrishnan adds 'wholeness': the integration that unites all values and organizes all experience. Such freedom and integration is what makes personhood, and 'being in the spirit' is the open and free reaction of the whole person – body, mind and spirit – to reality as a whole. So simple.

Clear perception of reality is crucial to the life of the spirit, and a poet's view can help to sharpen the concept of untainted perception. C. Day Lewis has written:

> It is thus that a poet is impressionable, developing a habit of mind which refrains, so to speak, from imposing on the outer world any pattern, formula or preconception, and is therefore able to see things as they really are.

In Day Lewis's understanding then, the true artist strips away all the associations of purpose, habit and use, which is how objects are usually defined and seen, in order to see the actual reality of an object, to see things as they really are. A chair is not simply viewed as something to be sat upon, or that stands in a particular place, or has a particular value, but its essential structure is seen; its uniqueness, its aesthetic worth and its sentimental import are all recognized. Then the chair is really seen, the reality of the particular chair grasped, and in this way things are seen 'as they really are'; and how similar this is to what we saw previously about empathic awareness.

It would seem therefore that the concept of what is real is fundamentally important to an understanding of spiritual connectedness. Indeed Radhakrishnan would say that spiritual connectedness is simply what occurs when what is real and unconstrained within is in contact with what is real and untainted without (recalling Kepler's dictum that to know is to compare that which is externally perceived with inner ideas and to judge that they agree). A similar view to this is held by Buber, and here we begin to find an important conjunction of ways of understanding what is real. Buber suggests that the basic paradigm of such experience (of what is real) is the spontaneous, free relationship which occurs between mother and child when they are with each other in open communion. In the connection between mother and baby, as there emerges a dawning recognition by both of the agency of the other, there naturally develops a relationship of tender reciprocity – mother and baby in tune in their separateness, knowing each other, touching each other, being totally real with each other. This development is natural and inevitable, provided nothing gets in the way, and it is this tender reciprocity, this free and open, loving communion between mother and baby, that Buber sees as the doorway to the life of the spirit. Piaget has similarly described a special state of communion between mother and child, as the child plays in the presence of mother, with mother there as a non-intrusive presence requiring no acknowledgement or definition. Piaget writes: 'His activity is thus bathed in an atmosphere of communion – one might almost speak of the "life of union" to use the terms of mysticism.' Such communion is a whole-person relatedness which is completely natural and free of all contrivance, and it requires the terms of mysticism to do it justice.

While such experience is rooted in the very earliest experiences of relatedness, it can later be actualized and made manifest in a personal reciprocity in which there is also no contrivance, and in which each speaks from the truth of the self. Such is a true-self relatedness, which Buber refers to as dialogical encounter. It carries with it the gleam of the earliest experiences of true relatedness between mother and baby, but extends it into the present to touch the most developed levels of personal encounter, with each participant seeing the gleam in the eye of the other.

When it comes to relating to a person, the poetic view of the reality of an object can again help to clarify what is meant by seeing the reality of another. Seeing things as they really are involves developing the habit of mind that refrains from imposing any preconceptions or formulas on what is seen. Therefore the reality of another person is seen only when all projection, transference, prejudice, restricted vision and whatever else may distort awareness of another has been shed or corrected. Only when this is so, do we see the reality and uniqueness of another person, and only when the same principle is applied to seeing ourselves do we know the truth of ourselves – or, more realistically, get somewhere near to that, since this state of relationship, to the other or to one's self, is something to be sought for rather than something frequently attained, although those moments when we do really meet another are experiences that we can 'know' in an intuitive way, even if the quality of the experience is impossible to put into words.

For such a concept of true meeting or dialogical encounter to have any meaning and applicability in psychotherapy, however, it is necessary to put it in a psychodynamic context, and we will approach this by first looking at the psychoanalytic view of what is meant by reality. This is not an easy task, but a necessary one to undertake if the spiritual aspect of relationship is to be integrated with psychological understanding.

Psychoanalysis began its particular contribution to a concept of reality with Freud's definition of the 'reality principle' as being distinct and fundamentally different from the 'pleasure principle'. The baby, so this thinking goes, at first demands immediate satisfaction of its needs and maintains a sense of omnipotent control of the sources of satisfaction by means of hallucinatory wish-fulfilment. When the object (mother) is not immediately available to satisfy demands, then hallucinatory recall of previous satisfaction is used to maintain the illusion of immediate satisfaction. In time, however, the reality that immediate satisfaction cannot always be demanded, that sources of supply cannot be omnipotently controlled, has to be recognized in order for the baby to survive. To deal effectively with reality, the fantasies of omnipotence have to be relinquished, disillusionment has to occur and the 'pleasure principle' be abandoned as the prime *modus vivendi*. This view established a sharp distinction, possibly too sharp, between fantasy and reality.

This is an issue carefully examined from a psychoanalytic perspective by Rycroft, in his papers collected under the title *Imagination and Reality*. His position is stated in the following quote:

> The capacity for personal relations is not simply a matter of being able to use objects to satisfy libidinal wishes but is the ability to maintain a reciprocal relationship between self and object before, during and after the consummatory acts appropriate to the particular relationship – and to maintain a living psychical relationship with the object during its absence – it is the capacity to keep in contact or communication with objects that are realistically conceived and are recognizable as being separate from the self.

Realistic conception of objects is in this view an essential part of the process of obtaining satisfaction, and Rycroft goes on to say that the purpose of psychoanalytic treatment is to establish, restore or increase the capacity for object relations, and to correct distortions thereof.

It is from this basis that he examines the nature and significance of disillusionment, and he starts from the fact that in everyday speech there are two quite different meanings of the word disillusion. It is used to denote the discovery that things are not as they had been incorrectly imagined or hoped to be, but also to mean the loss of the ability to find value and interest in things as they actually are, the latter probably being the more common usage. He suggests that this ambiguity provides some confirmation for the idea, so central to the thought of Winnicott, that an element of illusion enters into realistic awareness of the world around, that there is *not* a sharp distinction between fantasy and reality (just as we have seen previously that imagination enters into empathic awareness of the real world). It is this element of illusion that gives vitality and value to the way the world is experienced.

Rycroft points out that this seeming paradox is resolved if it is kept in mind that disillusionment, in the Freudian sense, applies not to the totality of relationship but only to the drive component, and that wishes by nature always tend towards hallucinatory wish-fulfilment. When reality sense is in abeyance, as in sleep, or has not yet been firmly established, as in infancy, the presence of and investment in an hallucinated imago leads to at least temporary satisfaction.

These imagos, as Rycroft refers to them, are the same as Stern's concept of internal representations that form as a result of repeated interactions with objects, and which integrated memory coalesces into a prototypical experience that can be evoked when mother (the object) is not present to give immediate satisfaction. At other times, however, when awake and after reality sense has been established, reality must prevail, but not all illusion is lost. Rycroft writes:

that Winnicott and Milner have in mind the idea that development of a healthy erotic relationship with reality involves that at the moment of consummation of a wish there should be a convergence and merging of the hallucinated imago with the imago of the external object.

In other words, at the time of consummation the reality of the external object is not altogether lost but is fused with the internal imago. Therefore, there is an illusory component but the object is still real. Here again is the importance of the fit between the internal world and the external, between the inner representation of an object and the object itself, and such a fit leads to freedom from the belief that desire and reality are in inevitable opposition. It leads to the development of a creative relationship with the world around, to a feeling of vitality and value in the way the world is experienced.

Rycroft next addresses the question of the necessary conditions for such a relationship to develop. Freud's hypothesis that in states of instinctual tension the infant tends to hallucinate memories of past satisfactions assumes that the infant has had such experiences, that its instinctual drive to seek satisfaction has been released and that a degree of correspondence beween the infant's latent impulses and what mother provides has been established. Rycroft says:

> Insofar as the mother arouses the infant's libidinal expectations and maintains them by a modicum of satisfaction, its perception and conception of reality will accord to the pattern of its inherent instinctive tendencies, and impulses will not merely tend to be subjectively felt to be good but actually will be developmentally bound to the imagos of the reality that released them. An imaginative sense of reality will develop which is stable because its development is part of the infant's self-realization.

Here Rycroft is not only correcting the too sharp distinction between fantasy and reality established by Freud, but in describing the particular fit between mother and child necessary for the grounding of the self is anticipating some of the ideas of Self Psychology. He emphasizes the importance of a true reciprocity, and this is both in keeping with, and gives a genetic base to, the importance of empathy as expounded by Kohut, as well as to dialogical encounter as formulated by Buber.

This would seem to be an important conjunction to reach, an agreeable meeting between psychoanalysis, Self Psychology and existentialism, and in addition it provides psychological support for the awareness of reality involved in spiritual connectedness. Reciprocity again has central significance. Essentially Rycroft is saying that an imaginative sense of reality develops when there is a fit between the infant's biologically based libidinal expectations and mother's response, and when such a fit can extend into other ways and avenues of relating. The disillusionment of Freud applies only to the libidinal part of that interaction.

Similar issues of fantasy and reality apply in the world of selfobjects as in the drive aspect of relatedness. At the beginning, for the object to function as a selfobject there must be the certainty of its presence, either in reality or in fantasy, and any sense that it is not so is experienced as a threat. As development proceeds, however, and the self achieves some strength and cohesion, then the object of the experience can become more abstract; symbolic representation may suffice for a time. Just as instinctive development extends beyond the imagos that release it into a creative sense of reality, as suggested by Rycroft, so can experiences of attunement, which are the grounds of selfobject experience, be extended by the child's imagination into creating symbols that carry the meaning of the experience.

The child is able to use an object to represent the holding or mirroring of the selfobject. At first mother must never be far away. As time goes by, however, while her immediate presence is largely necessary for mirroring, her comforting and strengthening functions become less dependent on her actually being there. And, as this development continues, not only does selfobject experience become more abstract but in time transcendent as well: the quality of extension beyond the world of immediate reality develops and a permanent place in the being of the child is established. In this way an inner world is created that can hold and sustain the self.

To see the full significance of this view of selfobject experience examples are needed, and the poet Wordsworth provides marvellous material for that. Wordsworth certainly had the clear vision of reality that we have come to see as important in spiritual connectedness; as *he* put it, he learned to see 'into the life of things'. He also had a deep awareness of self, which he particularly explored in his longer poems, in the prelude to one of which he refers to the mind of man as 'the main region of my song'. But in addition to this he presents wonderful poetic material for extending selfobject experience into transcendency.

Wordsworth lost both of his parents when he was a boy, and the intense relationship he developed to the world of nature, which is such a vital part of his poetry, can be seen as having provided compensation for these losses.

In the absence of his parents, nature came to have a very important selfobject function, and his poetry shows how this came about.

His intense empathic engagement in the world around is made clear in 'The Prelude' in the words:

> To every natural form, rock, fruit or flower,
> Even the loose stones that cover the highway,
> I gave a moral life – I saw them feel
>   or linked them to some feeling.

He also defines the fundamental fit or attunement with the experiential world that is the soil in which the self grows:

>   that calm delight
> Which if I err not, surely must belong
> To those first-born affinities that fit
> Our new existence to existing things.

The fit between new existence and existing things is precisely the fit between mother and child that Rycroft stipulated as the necessary ground for the development of a creative engagement in life, and it brings calm delight.

Wordsworth's mother, whom he described as having faith in the intrinsic nature of her children, and whom we can therefore assume to have been a good selfobject to her children, died when he was aged 8. His father died four years later. He also lost contact with his much-loved sister following his father's death. That particular experiences helped to sustain him following these losses is indicated in these lines from 'The Prelude':

> There are in our existence spots of time,
> .That with distinct pre-eminence retain
> A vivifying Virtue, whence . . .
>   our minds
> Are nourished and invisibly repair'd.

Whereas this language may be strange to us now, there could be no clearer description of experience of a selfobject than that it provides vivifying virtue; how important this must have been to the boy so touched by death and loss. How much he must have needed to be nourished and invisibly repaired.

As a boy Wordsworth experienced nature as a 'presence', and at times an experience that was so intense that, in his own words, '[it] would overspread my soul, that bodily eyes were forgotten'. One could say that it became a mystical experience. And at times this 'presence' would speak to him. Often, as a boy, of an evening at dusk when all was quiet, he would go to the lakeside and use his hands to make a hooting noise to get a response from the owls across the lake. Often there was no response, only silence, but on occasions:

> in that silence, while he hung
> Listening, a gentle shock of mild surprise
> Has carried far into his heart the voice
> Of mountain torrents.

'Mountain torrents' are Wordsworthian symbols for the language of nature, for the peculiar and profound meaning such experiences had for him. The boy was really spoken to in the silence.

We can imagine that experiences such as these did help to sustain him during those desperately lonely years of childhood, and also helped to produce a magical quality in some of his poetry. That Wordsworth understood the nature of what we are calling selfobject experience is particularly evident in 'The Two April Mornings'. It tells the story of an old man and a boy setting out for a walk in the hills. On the way the man is reminded of a day many years ago when he had visited his daughter's grave, and, turning away, he saw a beautiful girl who reminded him of his daughter. To see such a girl was a delight:

> 'No fountain from its rocky cave
> E're tripped with foot so free;
> She seemed as happy as a wave
> That dances on the sea.'

That the memory of his daughter had been awakened by the girl the following lines make clear:

> 'There came from me a sigh of pain
> Which I could ill confine;
> I looked at her and looked again:
> – And did not wish her mine.'

The old man was painfully reminded of his daughter, but he did not have to possess the girl for her to be part of his selfobject world. His selfobject experience was free of archaic bonds and, although it brought him pain it also brought some joy, and some poetic magic, for it was probably Wordsworth's daughter too.

In another poem, 'The Fountain', such selfobject extension could not occur. In this poem the same old man, Matthew, and the young are having a friendly talk by a fountain. The young man encourages the old to sing some mirthful songs to 'match/This water's pleasant tune'. But the old man is caught in thoughts of when he was young, and his eyes are dimmed with tears as he remembers all those dear to him who are now dead. The young man attempts to console him by saying:

> 'And, Matthew, for thy Children dead
> I'll be a son to thee!'
> At this he grasped his hands, and said,
> 'Alas! that cannot be.'

As they walk away from the fountain the old man sings some of the songs his friend had asked for, but there is no joy in his heart. This had not been a sustaining selfobject experience. It had brought only the artifice of gladness.

It was in 'Lines written a few miles above Tintern Abbey' that Wordsworth carried the awareness of nature of his boyhood most fully into transcendency and the expression of an intense spirituality. He had been in the same area, on the banks of the river Wye, five years previously, and the poem begins with reflections on how his memories of his previous visit had helped to sustain him through what had been five years of great tribulation. They had brought 'tranquil restoration' in 'hours of weariness' during those years. But also, by association with other remembered experiences of kindness and love, they produced:

> that blessed mood . . .
> In which the heavy and the weary weight
> Of all this unintelligible world
> Is lighten'd.

The experiences had come to have a strengthening effect as well as a calming one, and led to something of even greater moment, to a sense of becoming 'a living soul' suspended in the body, and:

> While with an eye made quiet by the power
> Of harmony, and the deep power of joy,
> We see into the life of things.

Thus, this developing selfobject experience, which began with the memory of his previous visit and by association extended to other good experiences, had not only at times been calming and strengthening, but also, despite the adverse circumstances, led to a consolidation of the self and to a deepening sense of being spiritually in tune with natural life.

Later in the poem he recalls how the invigorating impact of the immediate experience was all that mattered on the first visit, but now the high-spirited time of youth had gone, although the loss brought abundant recompense:

> For I have learned
> To look on nature, not as in the hour
> Of thoughtless youth, but hearing oftentimes
> The still, sad music of humanity,
> Not harsh, nor grating, though of ample power
> To chasten and subdue. And I have felt
> A presence that disturbs me with the joy
> Of elevated thoughts; a sense sublime
> Of something far more deeply interfused,
> Whose dwelling is the light of setting suns,
> And the round ocean, and the living air,
> And the blue sky, and in the mind of man.

Here, in this marvellous poetry, from our point of interest the words 'and in the mind of man' are of particular significance, making clear as they do that Wordsworth is indeed speaking of selfobject experience and not of anything supernatural. And we can fill this out further by looking again at the indications of how this was used in a compensatory way, first of all in relation to the loss of his parents, particularly his mother.

Jonathan Wordsworth affirms that the poems 'Michael' and 'The Ruined Cottage' are about refusal to admit despair. In these poems the poet indicates the intimate connection for him between places and people, and the need he has for consoling attachment to places, but also the unease he feels if they do not have a human connection. He records the experience of suddenly finding himself in an alien place and being reassured by signs of people having been there. This is how the poet describes it in 'The Ruined Cottage':

> If, looking around, I have perchance perceived
> Some vestiges of human hands, some stir
> Of human passion, they are to me as sweet
> As light at daybreak –

It is as if mother's presence must be preserved. The poem tells the simple, tragic story of the loving devotion of Margaret pining for the return of her lost husband, then losing her children and finally dying in despair. The very sad tale seems to have a cathartic effect on the poet

who ends up 'a better and a wiser man'. The cottage in ruins and the
deserted garden are central symbols, and Jonathan Wordsworth writes:

> By the end of the poem . . . the poet has come to a state of mind in
> which he too can stand back and trace the secret spirit of humanity.

Signs of Margaret's continuing presence in the ruin are a reassurance.
For places to be effective selfobjects to the poet they require the touch
of a woman's hand.

Yet, although such selfobject experience may at first have been
compensatory, it led ultimately to some deep realizations about life, and
a natural spirituality which may only have been spoiled by the later
commitment to the traditional Christian beliefs of the time.

It also led the poet back to the importance of personal relationships.
The years after the time when he first visited the region of the river Wye,
like those following the death of his parents, were ones of great
adversity during which relationship with nature was again used in a
compensatory way. However, by the time the lines above Tintern Abbey
were written, the selfobject experience had taken on a truly spiritual
quality and, with that, it not only provided the stabilizing effect of such
experience but also led back to human relationships, as the poet says,
'softened with the need for holy tenderness'. The following lines were
also probably written in 1798:

> Not useless do I deem
> These quiet sympathies with things that hold
> An inarticulate language, for the man
> Once taught to love such objects as excite
> No morbid passions, no disquietude,
> No vengeance and no hatred, needs must feel
> The joy of that pure principle of love
> So deeply that unsatisfied with aught
> Less pure and exquisite he cannot choose
> But seek for objects of a kindred love
> In fellow-natures, and a kindred joy.

It is possible that the power of this experience was subsequently lost to
the poet, and the loss may have contributed to the decline in quality of
his later poetry. But it still seems important to recognize clearly what he
found, and we may now be better able to see the significance of this.
In charting such a clear course from the 'first-born affinities that fit/
Our existence to existing things' to 'objects of a kindred love/In

fellow-natures' Wordsworth gives living substance to the development of selfobject experience; and recognition of the significance of self-object experience adds an extra dimension to Wordsworth's spirituality.

When this is added to the important conjunction we have already discovered between Rycroft's psychoanalytic understanding and the views of Kohut and Buber as they relate to the concept of reality and the world of the spirit, then the bridge between the psychological and the spiritual is greatly strengthened. It also, however, provides a bridge between the human and the divine, giving some reality to Radha-krishnan's 'the life divine in a body subject to sickness and death'.

It is interesting to note too the importance both Buber and Words-worth attach to tenderness, one to 'tender reciprocity' the other to 'holy tenderness'; this may have some real bearing on what is important in healing relationships.

Taking this material and this understanding into the confines of the therapeutic relationship, what can be said? First, that an extra dimension comes into the relationship at times when each participant senses and sees the reality of the other, and speaks from the truth of the self. Such is authentic relating, and for this to happen transference at the time must be transcended, all prejudice and wishful thinking be shed, all diss-embling and contrivance dropped. Such times of clarity can only be brief, but when they *do* happen, and to this is added an acknowledged mutual tenderness, then the spiritual side of a relationship starts to grow, and such growth tends to stabilize and strengthen the self so that the potential for reciprocity increases. The stronger the self, the greater is the possibility of reciprocity.

Just as Wordsworth was able to use his memories of a previous visit to the river Wye to sustain himself during some very difficult years, so a patient or client can use times of spiritual connectedness in therapy in a self-sustaining way. And then, as Wordsworth was able to expand the experience into an enduring and truly spiritual awareness of trans-cendency, so can a client or patient expand the self-strengthening quality of the relationship into a spiritual sense of the whole of reality; into selfobject experience which encompasses the whole of existence. What the consequences of such a development are, what difference it makes to both participants, is not easy to see or say. It requires some sense of the spirit in action, which is the subject of the next chapter.

Chapter 8

The spirit in action

The activity of the spirit is a mystery which is difficult to penetrate with our present modes of thinking, contaminated as they are by so much magical thought and superstition, and by much mystification of all kinds. It is indeed difficult to give such activity objective reality, to be able to demonstrate the difference 'being in the spirit' can make to a person's life. I am going to attempt this difficult task by recounting a personal journey: my own journey in relation to the life and work of New Zealand writer Janet Frame.

Her story is a remarkable one. After many years as a patient in mental hospitals, under the worst possible conditions, she recovered sufficiently to be able not only to leave hospital and live a full life but also to go on to become a writer of distinction.

In 1965 I went to work as a doctor at the hospital where Janet Frame had been a patient for most of the eight years she was in hospital. At the time she was starting to get some recognition as a writer, but, having myself just arrived in the country, I at first knew little about this and nothing whatsoever of her story. Gradually, however, I began to realize that here was something important. I learned that she had been diagnosed as schizophrenic and had spent considerable periods of time in wards for the more difficult and more deteriorated patients. I also became aware that there was unease among the staff about her. The novel *Faces in the Water*, which is based on her hospital experience, had been published two years previously, so it had only recently been having its impact on the staff of the hospital, some of whom were recognizable as characters in the book. I realized from the angry reactions of people that these characterizations were not felt to be complimentary. But it was some time before I got round to reading *Faces in the Water* and her earlier novel *Owls Do Cry*. That was when my amazement really began. I was immediately gripped by the question of how someone who had survived what she had been through could write so well about her experience.

I was learning each day something of what it had been like for her in hospital, because I was going into the wards where she had been and finding the conditions so awful that I could bear to be there for only short periods of time. *She* had endured such conditions for months on end. But there was more to it than that. She had left the hospital ten years previously, and conditions had been much worse then, and I knew what that had been like too. I had worked in a mental hospital in Scotland in 1955 and what I had experienced then, which was so bad as to be beyond any powers of description of mine, is what Janet Frame would have experienced, day in and out, months on end.

So this person had experienced the most dehumanizing and destructive social conditions imaginable over long periods of time and not been emotionally and spiritually destroyed by the experience. How could she have survived the ordeal, how was her spirit not destroyed, and how could she subsequently have found the mental strength and generosity of spirit to write so well about her experiences? These were the questions to which there seemed no easy answer and from which my journey started.

Never having had access to her clinical records, it was only when I read her three autobiographical books, on which the film giving her international recognition was based, that I became aware of the full magnitude of the problem of understanding her recovery. The horrors of the hospital years were by no means all that she had suffered. She had grown up in the depression years in a very poor family. The deprivations were great and were compounded by her brother suffering from severe epilepsy and, later, by two of her sisters dying by drowning, the first when Janet was still at school. In addition, her adolescent and early adult years had been a torment of self-consciousness and self-doubt, of social inadequacy and of alienation. It was when she had started working as a teacher, and was having her first class inspection, that, after impulsively walking out of the classroom, she took the overdose which resulted in her first admission to hospital. This subsequently led to a state of total mental collapse and the diagnosis of schizophrenia.

The autobiography also revealed that, after finally being discharged from hospital in New Zealand (only at the last minute had she been saved from having a lobotomy which would certainly have destroyed her writing ability), she had gone to London and then to Spain on a writing scholarship. A stay at the Maudsley Hospital in London resulted in the firm conclusion that she had not suffered from schizophrenia. It also provided her with the necessary care to be able to shed the mantle of schizophrenia (which, she acknowledged, she had come to use as a protection) and to become sufficiently restored in life and spirit to be able to commence and pursue her writing career.

My interest and puzzlement about the story increased with everything that I learned, but amazement reached its peak when I learned from the autobiography further details of her hospital experience and the fact that she had had more than 200 electro-convulsive treatments. This person had been exposed to the worst living conditions imaginable over a long period, and subjected repeatedly to a treatment which is not only very frightening in the way it was then given, but which damages the brain when used a lot, and yet, despite it all, she was becoming a great writer. How could this be understood psychologically? What held her together during those years?

At first these were intriguing clinical questions, but, as time went by, and as I explored her writing for possible answers – and having her wonderful autobiographies made this much easier – it became more of a spiritual quest. I had the sense that here was not only something of great clinical interest but, more importantly still, possibly something of great spiritual value. It is the essential features of my journey in search of understanding which I now present.

First of all, let us get some idea of where this journey takes us. In *On the Edge of the Alphabet*, a novel which explores how far words can go, she refers to outer reality as 'the solid furniture of living', and asks the question whether in finding her way she should simply use herself as a white stick in that world or whether she should risk going into the darkness within. The latter is chosen because without self-knowledge one can only stumble blindly through life. Going into the darkness within, however, risks getting lost, or as she says 'falling away', but it is a risk that must be taken, and one which we must take if *we* wish to follow her. It is a journey into the abyss. It is also one through what she refers to as 'the cold touch of death', the full significance of which we will see later. For these reasons it is not to be taken by the faint-hearted for it touches on one's own dark and dead place. In starting on such a journey it can help not only to have some idea of where it goes but something of the outcome as well.

I got the first clue to the survival of Janet Frame's mind and spirit from the title of her third autobiographical book, *Envoy from Mirror City*. Mirror City is a marvellous metaphor for the inner world of the self, the self in relation to its selfobjects, and with this clue I formulated the tentative hypothesis that she was able to survive because she could preserve intact the inner space she had so carefully cultivated during her adolescent and student years. While in hospital this space was her sanctuary.

As regards her restoration, which we are also interested in, what emerged as a possible explanation was that she was able to regain strength of mind and spirit because of her deep understanding of the healing power of grief, supported by her ability to confront death unambiguously; to know and to do that, and then be able to write about her experience, was, I concluded, what brought her restoration.

It is likely, however, that another factor helped her recovery, which was that there had been some real richness and security in her early years, the experience of which she vividly describes in her first autobiographical book, as was noted in the Prologue. The significance of this is made clear in the second part of the trilogy which has as its first chapter a single paragraph entitled 'The Stone'. In this paragraph she speaks of the future as an accumulating weight upon the past. Drawing on her own experience, she describes how the weight upon the earliest years is easiest to remove, allowing time to spring up again like green grass that has been lightly crushed. In contrast, the years following childhood become closely knit to the future, a massed weight which it is much more difficult to move. Beneath this weight the earlier time lies in a much more damaged state, like the white, twisted strands of grass one finds under a stone which has long been in position.

The crush of adversity began for Janet Frame in her early adolescent years. Because of the greenness of her early years, however, when the stone was lifted amazing regeneration could take place. Later, and in contrast to this, we will look at a character in one of her books who also lifted the stone of adversity but who on doing so found there was no life left, and died. Janet Frame lived, and the outcome she demonstrates, and which can be a help in facing the darkness, is that with a strong inner world one not only survives but can do so creatively.

With this information to assist us we can now explore her writing in more depth. The first important thing to see is that her view of the self fits well with Self Psychology. This is headlined by the titles of the autobiographies. *To the Is-land* is the emergence of the self. The angel of *An Angel at my Table*, the second book, is the selfobject presence that establishes and consolidates the self, while the envoy of *The Envoy from Mirror City*, the third, is the self that goes out into the world with a well-established inner world.

We also find that Janet Frame was well aware of the importance of the sort of experience we are calling selfobject experience. In the novel *Intensive Care* she gives a fine description of a selfobject. The central character of that novel, Millie, is simple-minded and almost certain to be classified as not sufficiently human, and disposed of somehow, when the Human Delineation Act comes into effect. Millie's immediate concern, however, is not that, but the pear tree in the garden. A large branch has been blown off in a storm and father has said that the tree must come down. Millie feels threatened by this because the tree is so important an object and place to her. Being under it feels like being under a 'considerate creature'. It is a place where she can 'just be', and a place where she feels safe. She thinks of other places, but none of them mean anything like so much to her as the Livingstone pear tree. She says you cannot leave part of yourself in other places because if you did and went away it would be gone when you returned, but not so with the tree. With it you could go away and what you left would still be there. The pear tree had become a guardian of the self, a selfobject, and Janet Frame describes finding in her own development a particular place for her self, at the age of 3 when her family moved to a new area. It was a place entirely her own, not to be competed for with her brother and sisters. And the experience of having her own unique place brought with it a sense of excitement in the world around, the confidence to start explor-ing her surroundings, in time to develop a strong passion for the solid furniture of living. Here we clearly see the self-strengthening effect of selfobject experience being described, and this is a small indication that we may be on the right lines.

The understanding I had come to was that, by the time of the collapse that resulted in her first admission to hospital, Janet Frame had developed such an intense and vital inner world that she was able to preserve that space intact during the terrible years in hospital, and was able to do so despite having virtually no human connectedness to support her, nor a place she could call her own. All that she had to hang on to was something that was very personal: a bag containing a book which she carried with her everywhere.

To make this thesis at all convincing, however, it is necessary to see in more detail what she had to survive in addition to her hospital experience. There was also what she refers to as the cold touch of death: her brother's epilepsy and the drowning of her sisters. Older sister Myrtle's death occurred when Janet was waiting to start High School. Following Myrtle's death, Janet found great consolation in poetry and solace in learning about ancient history and vanished cultures. She withdrew into history, culture and literature, and into writing poetry, which she had started some years previously but which took on parti-cular significance at this time. She became amazed at the marvellous knowledge of the poets, who, she felt, knew of Myrtle's death and could see into her own life. However, although this helped to stabilize her, and surely was the beginning of Mirror City, the self-created mirroring selfobject world, it did not remove the destructiveness of the loss. When at school she came to read of 'myrtles brown' in Milton's poem 'Lycidas' she describes how it had such an effect on her that she had to clench her toes and grip the desk with her hands to stop herself from bursting into tears.

Although it relieved some of the pain, and helped to hold her together, this way of dealing with her sister's death meant that the inner world was cultivated and strengthened but at the expense of her becoming increasingly shut off from her peers. Her years as a university student were ones of great isolation and alienation, during which she continued to cultivate her inner world. Rilke, the supreme poet of inwardness for whom fullness of being was the experiencing of the completest possible inner intensity, became one of her favourite poets. And in *Owls Do Cry* there is an indication that she was aware of the significance of this process. When she writes of her young sister Francie going to work at the mill she expresses the wish that Francie could have some 'treasure within her' to help her and that it were possible to tell what is treasure and what is not.

I suggest that, by the time her collapse came, she had developed such a rich inner world of treasure that it could maintain a thread of continuity of her being through all the terrible years of darkness in hospital. During that time, about the only thing she had to hold onto was the book of Shakespeare which she carried with her everywhere, in her bag. Referring to the importance of this book in *Faces in the Water*, she says that it was as if the book understood how things were; by its very presence it was a companion, and conferred on her the dignity of riches. How she needed those riches, and what an important selfobject the book had become.

During those years of darkness in hospital Janet Frame must have come to near-death of spirit. Her survival seems almost a miracle. But she needed not only to survive to do what she had to do. She needed restoration of mind and spirit, and I suggest that this came about by her confronting the darkness of death and then finding a light of renewal through expressing this in her writing. Here I believe we see the therapeutic value that writing can have.

While much of her writing explores the darkness of the inner world, and in doing so she confronts death with calmness and clarity, in the pursuit of light she can also reach out to life with hope and some

assurance, and in doing that she gives the impression of having discovered an inner truth, and acquired a perception of life that bears deep
wisdom. That, at least, is how I came to feel.

Janet Frame provides extensive material to illustrate the paradoxical
polarities of light and dark as each is given either a positive or negative
value. The predominant common-sense view is that light brings life out
of darkness. Light is the light of knowledge and darkness is ignorance.
But light is also the light of self-interest and self-will, and darkness the
ground of being, the source of fertility and creativity, the womb. We live
with the illusion that darkness is within and the light of reality is
without, but in truth a great darkness lies 'out there' in the cosmos, and
we live as individuals only by a tiny inner light.

These are some of the polarities that Janet Frames explores, and her
commitment is to the light of the imagination shining on the reality of both
life and death. In *Scented Gardens for the Blind* she writes of the shoulders
of men being bowed down by the weight of the light (of reality) which
despite its lack of pity is nevertheless an ally in man's war against death,
keeping up the illusion of meaning and substance.

In another novel, *The Rainbirds*, there is an emphasis on sunlight and
brightness, and the views that the city of Dunedin provides. But there is
also a dark side, the dark side of death, and the novel is about denial of
death and the attempt to gild the bed of death with light and about a
resurrection that proves lifeless.

When the central character, Godfrey, returns to the world from
having been declared dead, he attempts to re-establish himself in his
world of selfobjects: walking on his lawn, inspecting the garden, check-
ing his toolshed and being reminded by his store of paints with names
taken from the natural colours of the land of what a great place it was to
live, what a great land. Then daylight is described dying over Dunedin,
darkness coming down, but light still present in the western sky which
he attempts to track down. For Godfrey, however, the light proves
lifeless, and Frame writes that he knew without hope that it would
always elude capture.

For Janet Frame the light of Spain proved more life-giving than the
light of Dunedin. During her eight years in hospital she came to know
near-death of spirit. In her recovery Dunedin provided the first glimpse
of the possibility of renewal, of a light to be pursued, and of the Mirror
City, but it required a faraway light to restore her. Her restoration came
in Spain and in London. On the island of Ibiza she found a place where
the tideless ocean created a mirror she looked upon each day, where her
wish to be a writer became a reality and where she first fell in love.

Having had such experience as this, it is not surprising that the theme of resurrection appears frequently in her writing.

Later in *The Rainbirds* she explores another important dimension of the inner world – depth. As Godfrey tries to take up life again, he has to struggle to find a space in which his thoughts can live. Having been so near to death, his thoughts have difficulty in finding their place in the ordinary affairs of living. He experiences the routine of life and procession of seasons as invitations to oblivion. He feels an outsider but at the same time 'in deep', having been as far 'in' as a man can go and having come back again. He had been where everyone goes in the end but where many try to pretend that it is not so, covering the reality of death with a pleasant green camouflage.

Having been to that place herself, Janet Frame can take us unambiguously into the depths, into the darkness of death, but she does so not as an end but more as a beginning. She weaves words that lead towards life, and her courage and genius provide a shining example of new life arising out of near-death.

But she is clear how destructive death can be, and writes of this very forcefully in *Daughter Buffalo*. There she points out that with the advent of radio and television people have become exposed to more deaths than they can cope with. The written word gives more choice, allows one to take death in smaller doses, but the moving picture carries us straight to the scene. As a result we carry, she suggests, impressions of death, visions of the dying, which are so many and so ill-defined that we are unable to deal with them, because we do not have the necessary feelings to match them. There is not adequate time for grief and mourning. The deaths have no silence in which to become real. As a consequence of this poverty of feeling, in the face of continuing exposure, feelings turn to hate. In the end, having nothing left to give to the demands of death, we give ourselves; we become death.

Yet in the same book she uses the image of the silkworm feeding on death and, in dying, producing strands of silk. Based on that image she gives a vivid picture of the healing power of grief. To be effective grief is often noisy and can go on all night when the rest of the world is sleeping, but if it is allowed time to do its work it can unravel all the torment and the toil and eventually produce a 'golden trophy'. Here, in her powerful writing, comes through her faith in life, and here she demonstrates how creative writers can provide powerful images and metaphors of healing. For those who can grieve, for those who are in touch with the natural processes of life there is a golden trophy, there is healing.

In another novel, *The Adaptable Man*, it is the simple country people, solidly embedded in their immediate surroundings, who really live and know the reality of death, and who are in touch with the natural processes of life. The people Frame sees them to resemble most are the mental patients, whom she describes in vivid and earthy language as being those who are completely dissatisfied with the world of commerce and industry, and whose dissatisfaction leads them to a dream world where they are close to nature and unconcerned about social constraints. If they speak much at all it is to the slow pace of natural processes, in time with the seasons that 'breed, nurse, destroy and resurrect them'. Who could doubt that Janet Frame is speaking here of her own experience of dying and returning to life. Characters in the book other than the simple folk are lifeless, living in a world of illusion, phantoms flitting across the stage of life.

All, that is, except Aisley Maude, the confused clergyman whose image of God had lost all focus but who now senses God as a miracle of engineering precision. This vision came to him when, cured of tuberculosis but without hope of a loving relationship, he had gone into solitude 'to stare at the meaning of being', as Janet Frame has accepted solitude in pursuit of creative work. With the new sense of God he discovered, could he be indulging in the fantasy that grace, if it is allowed to work, is precise and powerful in the promotion of the self, and could this be the living stream that Janet Frame found? It is a possibility that another poet, Wallace Stevens, pointed to when he wrote 'that the imagination is a miracle of logic, and that its exquisite divinations are calculations beyond analysis'.

While it is clear that Janet Frame is writing out of her own experience here, particularly her struggle to find a place for herself in life after her illness, she may also be pointing to a psychological reality which is generally applicable; and that is that in the depths of being resides a primordial fear of death, not so much fear of death as an end-point but more a dread of abandonment and failure of being. Getting into such depths of experience may be so disturbing that most people avoid it, covering it with a green carpet of routine living. It is to that dreadful place that her journey takes us, however, and in doing so it touches that place in our own experience, or in our imagination, if we allow it.

If we have been to that place, however, and returned, does the experience have a particular value? Does resurrection from such a place, and the deeper sense of reality it brings, carry with it an intuitive sense of life that can be as precise and logical as the instrumentality of science, and can this be the basis of a natural spirituality? These are the questions that Janet Frame finally raised for me on my journey, and to which I will now try to give an answer.

A further version of the life out of death theme, and the search in solitude for the self, is explored by Frame in the novel *A State of Siege*. Here the central character, a woman, Malfred, has been freed by her mother's death, and by retirement from school teaching, and chooses to go into a life of solitude where she can be 'free, in charge and at rest'. These are important to her because till now her experience, and her view of life, have been blocked by the closeness of demanding relatives, particularly caring for her mother, and possession by the routine and the trivial in teaching. She has had little opportunity to be herself. On the first night in her new home, however, Janet Frame has her realizing that death is too cold a touch to be used for release into life, as well as becoming aware of the absence of a loving touch. In this state she has a dream 'of a vast imaginative force, that quells prejudice, suspicion, that acts as a beam to draw different countries close, so that each seeks, with instructive vision, the needs of the other'. Could there be a more hopeful or spiritual dream, and could there be a clearer statement of the part imagination plays in empathic relatedness and of what a difference that can make not only in a personal sense but in a political one too?

Although it has allowed her a new view, the touch of death has not released Malfred from old selfobject experiences in time to make new ones. There is no loving touch. Yet she is determined to break down the old, and during a terrible night of storm she goes into the darkness of herself, and experiences a fearful knocking and breaking down and being broken into, as if the storm were destroying her. In this terror she is eventually able to return in her imagination to the beloved river country of her childhood, that is to what little sustaining selfobject experience she has left, but it is not enough and she dies.

In this dramatic and concrete way Frame has her suffer the turmoil of lifting the stone that crushed her spirit, but finding, having done so, that there is insufficient life left. Malfred's release came too late. There was not enought in her inner world to sustain her. There was no love. When she got to the essence of herself there was only silence.

Fortunately for us, Janet Frame found at that place not only the courage and strength to stay alive but also a distinctive voice with which she could give eloquent utterance in her writing. This we can now review in an attempt to further amplify the answers to the questions raised.

I believe that abstracted selfobject experience did indeed sustain her through her ordeal, and that this experience allowed her to recognize clearly the importance of grief in the growth of the self, and that such growth through grief leads to a spirituality with self-expanding and self-strengthening qualities. There would seem, however, to be an extra dimension beyond the purely psychological required to understand her life and work, and I suggest that this extra dimension is the spirit in action. Not only does this help us to understand what seems to defy rational understanding, it also has an impact if hearts and minds are opened to it. It brings upliftment of spirit.

Janet Frame's autobiography makes clear that during her eight years in hospitals in New Zealand she had no personal relationships of any significance, and she lost all effective contact with her family. During adolescence, and particularly at the time of the death of her sister, she used poetry and her embeddednes in literature, as well as love of writing, to sustain her. There would seem to be little other than this that could have sustained her during those years. Can we presume then that, as a consequence of being able to preserve her inner space inviolate, not only could her spirit survive, but her poetic imagination continue to operate as well? The poignant descriptions of some of her fellow patients in *Faces in the Water* are certainly drawn with such empathy and skill as to suggest that she was in creative contact with her surroundings, despite the conditions she was living under. Does the creative process in this way have a special quality and special requirements, and does this again demonstrate the life and action of the spirit?

In his *Beethoven Essays*, on the subject of Beethoven's deafness, Maynard Solomon writes:

> Beethoven's music came to maturity in a silent space carved out of his own body, perpetually secluded, and in permanent symbiosis with a nourishing female principle. An inner darkness that has the double significance of birth and death also supplied the ground for a creativity that partook of opposed generative forces.

This quotation could equally well apply to Janet Frame. The significance that Solomon gives to the life–death polarity is particularly interesting. From this we can get some confirmation for the idea that Janet Frame was able to preserve a 'silent space' which not only sustained but added to her creative powers and generated great wisdom. It is here that the concept of selfobject has an explanatory value, psychologically, that has previously been lacking. It offers a way of understanding how inner space can support and sustain the self, and provide, along with the instrumental dimensions of the exercise of autonomy, a bridge into the life of the spirit.

There is no need for further clarification of the significance Janet Frame attaches to the grief process, but to restate it briefly: in the self's confrontation with death and the experience of loss, and with the existential reality of failure, with its nihilistic encounter that can destroy purpose, it is grieving that can bring back life and strength.

Some amplification of this might help, however, and can be found in the work of another poet who also got to the doors of death in the extremity of depression: Alfred Tennyson. This amplification allows another important step to be taken: with Tennyson we can find love more clearly instated as a significant part of the grieving process.

In 'In Memoriam', written when he was a young man in memory of his beloved friend Arthur Hallam who had died when abroad, he writes: 'Let love clasp grief lest both be drowned.' With the wonderful image of love clasping grief, we can feel a new dimension entering the grieving process. In the poem, when Arthur's body is brought back to England for burial there comes:

> would breathing through his lips impart
> The life that almost dies in me.

Here again we have the near-death experience, and later in the poem the well-known lines:

> This truth came borne by bier and pall,
>   I felt it when I sorrowed most,
>   'Tis better to have loved and lost
> Than never to have loved at all.

If indeed there is truth in this, that in facing death and encountering nihilistic fears there can be restoration and healing if both grief and love together do their work, there is further confirmation for our thesis.

What we are also sensing, however, is that Janet Frame takes us beyond restoration and healing. In suggesting that grief work can lead to a sense of attunement with life that is life-enhancing, and to a natural spirituality that involves being so in touch with life, so accurately tuned-in, that it gives direction and purpose to life, she is installing the inner guide to negotiate the solid furniture of living. And in doing so she is introducing ideas that lead to the recognition of selfobject experience that encompasses the whole of life and being, and both consolidates and expands the self.

This intensity of experience we have already found in Wordsworth, but here, in the life and work of Janet Frame, it is given a clearer psychological perspective and grounding. It seems to me that because of her intense encounters with death and madness there is something very special in her view, something that can be added to Eissler's opinion that a tendency towards psychosis is one of the prerequisites for great art. Another may be having the courage to encounter the touch of death unambiguously, and the strength to survive and be creative with it.

Janet Frame found a home for herself in language and literature, a place where she could be both guest and host. Outside her autobiographical writing, she is not simply an author of fiction but also the fiction of an author. She hovers on the interface between fact and fiction, between the world of reality and the world of the imagination, as we are hovering at this point between psyche and spirit. From that position she has developed a particular perspective. It is a detached perspective, but one that sees right into the nature of things, and this perspective transforms her loneliness. It is a detached perspective, but one that allows the transition from self-centred loneliness to the ability to be alone, aware of the world beyond oneself and the possibility of God.

Epilogue

Having completed this account of my journey I want now to draw together the important things I have learned and which follow from it.

I began the journey with the sense that for me there was something significantly lacking in the clinical approach of psychotherapy of the time, dominated as it was by psychoanalysis, with its emphasis on biological drive, and by analytic psychology, with the emphasis on the inner world of archetypes. The recognition of the clinical relevance of the self seemed to provide what was lacking, and to fill out personality into a true human-beingness that took into account the uniqueness of the experience of each individual. With the latter came the recognition that a relationship can be said to be personal only when it includes how each in their hearts and minds experiences the other.

During the journey I came to see that the life of the self is a two-stage process. We can only be true to 'our selves' when we know what that means, and we can only know that when we experience an interaction in which we are open and free, and which gives the feeling of being 'right for me'. The sense of who I am does not emerge spontaneously from within, but only when one is engaged empathically and reciprocally with an 'other' in a way that allows discrimination between what is truly 'right for me' and what is not. Having had that experience, it is then necessary to withdraw into oneself to allow the sense to be given firm inner definition. This two-stage process is the soil in which the true self grows, and empathy and reciprocity are at the core.

Crucial in the growth of the self is the adequacy of selfobject experience, and equally crucial to the establishment of mature relationships, as well as an intimate understanding of the world, is the experience of open and true reciprocity. Selfobject experience grounds the self. The current of reciprocity establishes selfhood socially and opens the door into the world of the spirit.

Along with this, I came to see that therapy also is a two-stage process. First there is the overcoming of the obstacle, the releasing of the internal block, the freeing from the self-destructive pattern of repeatedly playing out the original trauma without release. Following the release is the creative act: the replacement of the bondage to sorrow and fear by an active and imaginative assertion of individuality. First the healing, then the creation of conditions for self-growth, as well as the necessary exercise of the self imaginatively and creatively. And in this process it is mainly the personal presence of the other, the therapist, that heals and imparts wisdom, rather than the words that are spoken. Important personal qualities in therapy – integrity, sincerity, vitality, hopefulness – cannot be conveyed by words alone. Indeed, in truth, they may not be conveyed by words at all. In this way I have come to agree with Buber that 'regeneration of a stunted personal centre is only accomplished by someone who stands not only at his own pole but also at the other, experiencing the effects of his own action'.

When the self is given central place, the relationship between therapist and patient inevitably assumes crucial importance. Authentic meeting becomes an aim of therapy: *the* aim of therapy of the self. And there is nothing whatsoever new in this suggestion or realization. Indeed, such a point of view could not be better put than it was twenty-five years ago by R.D. Laing:

> Psychotherapy must remain an obstinate attempt of two people to recover the wholeness of being human through the relationship between them.
>
> Any technique concerned with the other without the self, with behaviour to the exclusion of experience, with relationship to the neglect of the persons in relation, with the individuals to the exclusion of their relationship, and most of all, with an object-to-be-changed rather than a person-to-be-accepted, simply perpetuates the disease it attempts to cure.
>
> And any theory not founded on the nature of being human is a lie and a betrayal of man. An inhuman theory will inevitably lead to inhuman consequences – if the therapist is consistent. Fortunately, many therapists have the gift of inconsistency. This, however endearing, cannot be regarded as ideal.

Thus, I have come to the view that the quality of the therapist's presence is as important in therapy as what techniques are used, and in addition there is the sense of there being a spiritual aspect to authentic meeting. This is a view that is now shared by one of the most respected of psychotherapy practitioners and researchers: Carl Rogers. As reported in *The Use of the Self in Therapy*, Rogers has this to say:

> I think that therapy is most effective when the therapist's goals are limited to the process of therapy and not to the outcome. I think that if the therapist feels 'I want to be present to this person as much as possible. I want to listen to what is going on. I want to be real in this relationship' then these are suitable goals for the therapist. If the therapist is feeling 'I want this person to get over his neurotic behaviour. I want this person to change in such and such a way' I think this stands in the way of good therapy.

He then goes on to say that his views have broadened into a new area:

> I would put it that the best of therapy leads to a dimension that is spiritual, rather than saying that the spiritual is having an impact on therapy. But it depends on your definition of spiritual. There are certainly times in therapy and in the experience I have with groups where I feel there is something going on that is larger than what is evident. I have described this in various ways. Sometimes I feel much as the physicists, who do not really split atoms; they simply align themselves in accordance with the natural way in which atoms split themselves. In the same way, I feel that sometimes in interpersonal relationships power and energy get released which transcends what we thought was involved.

What I think is particularly important to note here is the thought that the spiritual dimension is not something extraneous that has an impact on therapy, but a quality that emerges 'in the best of therapies'. It is an actual achievement in personal relationship which can be worked towards, and some of the possible ways and guides to how it can be achieved we have explored, and this is the basis of the claim that there can in fact be a therapy of the spirit.

However, as well as these realizations, there are also important social consequences that follow from giving the self central significance in psychological understanding. We live in a time not only of rapid change but also of increase in the shaking of the foundations of the established social structures and ways of construing the world. As was pointed out in the prologue, there is reason for thinking that the social foundations of the self may be weakening at the very time that self-realization is being given special importance. If this is so, we would expect to see that people are under strain, and the increasing level of violence and social turmoil certainly indicates that it is so. That the strain is particularly on the psyche is indicated by the amount of interest there is in psychological healing and personal growth, as well as the flood of literature on these subjects that is available. It may be, as Pirsig has suggested in his novel *Lila*, that a major change has been occurring in this century from behaviour being predominantly socially conditioned and controlled, as it was in Victorian times, to it being controlled intellectually, that is by individual thought, by the self. If this is so, and it is a convincing suggestion, the strains of the present time could be the result of going through a transitional phase of moving from what has been a theo-centric faith, with emphasis on external control and direction of moral behaviour, to a self-centred faith, with the emphasis on inner direction.

There are indications that such a change is in fact occurring in the religious world. The highly regarded poet and Trappist monk, Thomas Merton, said that what is essential to the monastic quest is to be sought in the area of true self-transcendence, in the transformation of consciousness in its ultimate ground. He wrote:

It is important that this element of inner transcendent freedom – this element of depth and integrity – be kept alive as we grow toward the full maturity of universal man. We are witnessing the growth of a truly universal consciousness in the modern world. This may be a consciousness of transcendent freedom or vision, or it may simply be a vast blur of mechanized triviality and ethical cliché.

If such a move to a self-centred faith is indeed occurring, what does it mean? And how can it be recognized? First of all it must be a move to being 'centred' on the inner world rather than the outer; on a belief that the true locus of moral and spiritual direction lies not in a God 'out there' but within the psyche; a faith in inner directedness and in the genius of the unconscious self. With this goes the faith in an internal prompting towards self-actualization, the accomplishment of which not only fulfils the built-in programme of human-beingness but also brings satisfaction and gives purpose to living. This is a faith in the process of individuation, and these are the fundamental values and beliefs that would constitute such a faith.

But also it would be a faith in the uniqueness of the authentic self, the true self: a belief that the power within is given a unique expression when the true self is actualized, and that such expression is the creation of the person who achieves it. (In parenthesis, I would say that I am doubtful whether this is solely self-creation and not also the operation of grace that simply comes to one. But, at least, the creative activity of the self is involved.) In this way, however, living the truth of oneself can be seen as a creative act, perhaps *the* creative act. But more than that. If there is in the 'power within' an evolutionary trend, if there is a gradual cultural process of increasing self-actualization, then extending one's self would be an act which promotes the whole evolutionary process of the emerging self. If this is the truth of existence, then every individual has the chance to play an important part in this the greatest of undertakings, and no one has put this idea more forcefully than Bernard Shaw. In *Man and Superman* Shaw has Don Juan say:

> I tell you that as long as I can conceive something better than myself I cannot be easy unless I am striving to bring it into existence or clearing the way for it. That is the law of my life. That is the working within me of Life's incessant aspiration to higher organization, wider, deeper, intenser self-consciousness, and clearer self-understanding.

Shaw is no doubt speaking his own mind here, and the working within he refers to is not simply a matter of fulfilling an in-built destiny, but gives life meaning and purpose, something to devote oneself to, something wonderfully well worth doing. It gives true joy in living, and Shaw demonstrated this in his life remarkably.

There is a feeling of religious fervour in Shaw's writing on Creative Evolution, and a self-centred faith would indeed be, in a sense, religious; but a religion without any creed or mythology or ritual or belief system other than the special significance given to the self. It does mean going beyond the evidence in affirming that self-development is essentially what life is about, and what can give life joy and satisfaction, but faith *is* being prepared to go beyond the evidence. It is a matter of conviction and commitment in giving a special personal and communal direction to life. These are religious attitudes, and there may be a possibility now of such an awakening, which Bernard Shaw was not able to spark despite his persuasive powers, because only now is self-knowledge sufficiently clear to give it firm ground.

If a move in this direction is occurring, or starting to occur, perhaps the clearest signs are coming from the women's movement. Here, there is not only a move into a strong emphasis on self-determination and human rights but also a move into a spirituality centred on the self. Women are speaking very clearly on this, and perhaps no-one has done so more clearly than Anais Nin in *A Woman Speaks*. In it she quotes with approval R.D. Laing's statement in *The Politics of Experience*:

> We all live in the hope that authentic meetings between human beings can still occur. Psychotherapy consists in the tearing away of all that

stands between us – the props, masks, roles, lies, anxieties, projec-
tions and introjections – in short, all the carry-overs from the past, the
transference and counter-transference, that we use by habit and collu-
sion, wittingly or unwittingly, as our currency for relationships.

In approving of Laing, Nin is emphasizing the part that therapy can play
in freeing people to be themselves, and in quoting Laing she is making
the point that therapists have moved beyond what many women had
come to criticize in Freud.

Authentic being is Nin's aim, and therapy a frequently necessary step
to getting there. Authentic being requires that one gives oneself to life to
the full, not in any sacrificial way, but simply in putting oneself out to
the best of one's ability and in making the best use of oneself. One of the
ways she found to support her in this undertaking, and it is of particular
interest in the light of some of the conclusions we have come to, was
daily writing of a personal diary. About this she writes:

> So I am speaking now of the diary – not as a work of literature but as
> something necessary to living, as a way of orienting ourselves to our
> inner lives. It doesn't matter in what form you do it, whether it's
> meditation, whether it's writing or whether it's just a moment of
> thoughtfulness about the trend, the current of your life. It is a moment
> of stopping life to become aware of it. And it's this kind of awareness
> which is threatened in our world today, with its acceleration and with
> its mechanization.

It was in her diary that she expressed the truth of herself, stayed true to
her core, while commenting on the manifold and sometimes chaotic and
decadent experiences of life she allowed herself. She said that she
created the diary because she needed a friend, and that it kept her alive
as a human being. Such is the importance that Anais Nin attached to
internal discourse as a means of centring and sustaining the self, the real
benefits of which came, one would feel, from her persistence in it.

However, not only is there a powerful movement towards self-
determination occurring among women, but also it would seem a strong
move into spirituality. To support this, and give some substance to it, I
am going to use an essay written by a friend: a woman and a poet.

In writing on *Poetry as Prayer*, Miriam Richardson explores the
correspondence between what Anderson and Hopkins in *The Feminine
Face of God* call prayer and what she experiences when writing poetry:

> There are three ways in which I write poems; there are ready-made
> poems; there are those in which I find and match words to a clearly

perceived experience; and finally, those which begin with a surface word or image, and by a process much like free association evolve into a poem.

She says the 'ready-made' poems come as a surprise, have an uncanny quality and tend to come complete. They have the 'unshakeable authority', according to Miriam, that Anderson and Hopkins found at times in prayer, which for them is 'the authentic voice from within which is part of the spiritual journey as one moves toward knowledge, understanding and acceptance of the inner, real, lived experience of one's own life'.

Here again is the emphasis on clarity and reality which we have come across previously as avenues of the spirit. Anderson and Hopkins see prayer as a means of living with one's essence, getting beyond the distortions of culture and upbringing and living authentically. Spiritual exercises are defined as 'any activity that is engaged in regularly and in depth with the intention of bringing one into direct experience of the real', and Miriam's second way of writing poetry is like that. It tries to give 'shape in words to clear, often powerful, experiences which have an integrity of their own'.

The third way 'involves taking the most immediate prominent feeling or image and exploring it; finding the right adjectives, following its lead into other images or feelings until a cohesive gestalt emerges – and it always seems to, if I can allow the flow its own direction'. This can be seen to be equivalent to the discernment that Anderson and Hopkins see as so necessary to ensure that inner guidance is not just another way to disguise the demands of one's ego. Discernment distinguishes what is true from what is false, and integrity is as important in art as it is in prayer, or so it would seem.

Not only is Miriam demonstrating in this way a similarity between her writing of poetry and prayerful meditation, her material also presents an interesting connection with the three stages of development of the self as defined by Stern. Her ready-made poems can be seen as expressions of the core self (the authentic voice from within); her second way of writing, the tuning-in of the intersubjective self which gives a direct experience of the real; and the third way is the 'matching of words to powerful experiences', which is the function of the verbal self.

It is also important, I think, to reflect on how this may bear on therapy, particularly as regards the importance of integrity. If the aim is authentic being, and if therapy is seen as the clearing away of all that gets in the way of this, then therapists must be clear about themselves in this regard, and take this very seriously. They must exercise the same integrity as is necessary in writing a poem or saying a prayer, and here again the spiritual can be seen to be entering into the therapeutic; and in doing so it introduces a moral dimension.

This can perhaps be seen more clearly if it is put in the context of Meares's two types of transference. The first is the selfobject transference in which, by maintaining an empathic presence, the therapist holds and nurtures the self of the other. Disruption of this state requires from the therapist acceptance of the transference distortions that occur, as well as the effort to understand and clarify what is necessary in order to restore the empathic bond. Disruption can also result, however, in a space in which two distinct selves can recognize and relate to each other, in an authentic meeting, and it is on this basis of person-to-person acknowledgement and respect that the moral aspect of the relationship can be grounded. Such a moral aspect, when it is well established, would allow no exploitation of the other, psychologically, sexually or in any other way.

Clear boundaries of behaviour have to be set in therapy, but these cannot be absolute without being constraining and constricting. Having a moral attitude, and this being cultivated by the therapist, and having a moral understanding, the development of which is part of the process of therapy, together allow the maintenance of right behaviour without the constriction of absolute rules.

Such a development can occur in a relationship, however, only by slow increments, and it is something to be gradually worked upon as is any other aspect of relating. It can be seen as similar to the development of the self, which happens only very slowly as 'islands of consistency' of experience gradually, over a long period of time, coalesce into a sustained sense of self. Likewise, as moments of authentic meeting gradually grow into an established spiritual bond, the moral dimension of the relationship becomes so well established that it can be the grounds for maintaining the rightness of behaviour.

Two crucial areas in therapy in which behaviour is particularly important are the extent of physical touching and the amount of self-disclosure by the therapist, and there is at present a lot of concern and confusion about both of these. As regards the former, physical touching as an expression of respect and concern must surely have its place, and its rightness can best be guided by the personal reciprocity, the authentic meeting, that we have been considering. What cannot have a place, if personal reciprocity is what counts, is active sexual contact, because when passion takes control then the on-going check of personal reciprocity is inevitably for the time lost. As regards self-disclosure, if being fully present is an important part of therapy, then it clearly has its place too. What matters here is that it is in the interests of the patient, and neither an unburdening nor an exhibitionistic exercise on the part of the therapist. Again it is more likely that this will be got right if the moral aspect of the relationship is well established, particularly when it is supplemented by mutual negotiation about what is right and wished for and appropriate.

When this is clear and solid, when such an understanding is firmly in place, then love, in whatever form it may take, apart from sexual contact, may safely play its part. For, as we saw in the last chapter, it may be when grief and love together do their work that the deepest changes in therapy occur. It may be that the important turnings that occur as a result of therapy are: from craving to creating; from looking to the outside to satisfy one's needs, be it from persons or from things, to looking to the inside; and from self-protection into openness and love.

The poet Rilke has said that love and art together seek to know otherness in all its immediate reality. We have come to see self therapy as a meeting with otherness, a particular form of connectedness. It may be that it too is at its most effective when love and art together do their work. A clear statement on integrity and connectedness would seem to be right at this point, and it is more than ever right that it should come from Lawrence who has been such a big influence on this journey. In *Lawrence's Men and Women* Sheila Macleod makes such a clear statement. She writes:

> The whole thrust of Lawrence's work is towards wholeness: the unity of being and of experience. This means not only the integrity of the microcosm which is a human being, but the integrity of the universe, the macrocosm of which the human being is inevitably a part. In seeing the modern world as fragmented and mechanical, Lawrence was accusing it of lack of integrity. For him order was not to be produced out of chaos through the workings of the mind, however rational, nor yet through the products of the mind, however technically perfect. On the contrary, order and meaning already exist in the universe and can be apprehended only through intuitive sympathy or blood-knowledge, a process from which modern men and women have alienated themselves. Because they are out of connection with themselves, they are also out of connection with one another, and hence with the whole series of shifting complexities which constitutes life as part of the natural world.

So, at the end of this long journey, we may find no more than, quoting Rogers, 'something going on that is larger than what is evident'. But it is also possible that it is something much bigger of which we have yet to start to see the full import, and with that possibility in mind I want to give the last word to George Steiner, the title of whose latest book, *Real Presences*, fits so well with our closing theme that therapy is so much a matter of presence. But I also do so because of his use of the word God. In the book he starts by addressing the matter of the persistence of the use of the word God, when there is no plausible reflection or belief to underwrite 'God's presence', nor any intelligible evidence to support it. He writes:

> Where God clings to our culture, to our routines of discourse, He is a phantom of grammar, a fossil embedded in the childhood of rational speech.

Having said that, however, he then goes on to argue the opposite. He proposes that the capacity of human speech to communicate meaning and feeling is itself, in the final analysis, underwritten by the assumption of God's presence; and that the presence of 'otherness' is a necessary ground for the experience of aesthetic meaning. In his words:

> that the wager on the meaning of meaning, on the potential of insight and response when one human voice addresses another, when we come face to face with the text and work of art and music, which is to say when we encounter the other in its condition of freedom, is a wager on transcendence.

Is this a wager that should now be taken in the therapeutic encounter with the other, and has it become a matter of urgency to do so?

Bibliography

Ackroyd, P. (1983) *The Last Testament of Oscar Wilde*. London: Hamish Hamilton.

Anderson, S. and Hopkins, P. (1991) *The Feminine Face of God*. New York: Bantam Books.

Auden, W.H. (1969) 'An improbable life', in R. Ellmann (ed.) *Oscar Wilde: A Collection of Critical Essays*. Englefield Cliffs, NJ: Prentice-Hall.

Buber, M. (1947) *Between Man and Man*. London: Collins.

Buber, M. (1970) *I and Thou*, trans. W. Kaufman. Edinburgh: T. & T. Clark.

Campbell, J. (1986) *The Inner Reaches of Outer Space*. New York: Harper Perennial.

Day Lewis, C. (1961) *The Poetic Image*. London: Cape.

Day Lewis, C. (1969) *The Buried Day*. London: Chatto & Windus.

Ellmann, R. (1987) *Oscar Wilde*. London: Hamish Hamilton.

Frame, J. (1957) *Owls Do Cry*. Christchurch (NZ): Pegasus Press.

Frame, J. (1961) *Faces in the Water*. Christchurch (NZ): Pegasus Press.

Frame, J. (1965a) *On the Edge of the Alphabet*. New York: Braziller.

Frame, J. (1965b) *Scented Gardens for the Blind*. Christchurch (NZ): Pegasus Press.

Frame, J. (1965c) *The Adaptable Man*. Christchurch (NZ): Pegasus Press.

Frame, J. (1966) *A State of Siege*. New York: Braziller.

Frame, J. (1969) *The Rainbirds*. Christchurch (NZ): Pegasus Press.

Frame, J. (1972) *Daughter Buffalo*. New York: Braziller.

Frame, J. (1979) *Living in the Maniototo*. New York: Braziller.

Frame, J. (1983) *To the Is-land*. London: The Women's Press.

Frame, J. (1984) *An Angel at my Table*. Auckland: Hutchinson Group (NZ).

Frame, J. (1985) *The Envoy from Mirror City*. Auckland: Hutchinson Group (NZ).

Frame, J. (1987) *Intensive Care*. Auckland: Hutchinson Group (NZ).

Herman, J.L. (1992) *Trauma and Recovery*. New York: Basic Books.

Holroyd, M. (1988) *Bernard Shaw: The Search for Love*. London: Chatto & Windus.

Holroyd, M. (1989) *Bernard Shaw: The Pursuit of Power*. London: Chatto & Windus.

Kohut, H. (1971) *The Analysis of the Self*. London: The Hogarth Press.

Kohut, H. (1977) *The Restoration of the Self.* New York: International Universities Press.

Kohut, H. (1984) *How Does Analysis Cure?* Chicago and London: University of Chicago Press.

Laing, R.D. (1967) *The Politics of Experience and the Bird of Paradise.* Harmondsworth: Penguin.

Lawrence, D.H. (1931) *Fantasia of the Unconscious.* London: Secker.

Lawrence, D.H. (1968) *Phoenix 11*, ed. W. Roberts and H.T. Moore. London: Secker.

Lawrence, D.H. (1981) *The Rainbow.* Harmondsworth: Penguin.

Lorenz, K. (1977) *Behind the Mirror.* London: Methuen.

Macleod, S. (1987) *Lawrence's Men and Women.* London: Paladin.

Meares, R. (1992) *The Metaphor of Play.* Sydney: Hill of Content.

Merton, T. (1973) *The Asian Journals of Thomas Merton*, ed. H. Burton, P. Hart and J. Laughlin. New York: New Direction Books.

Nin, A. (1992) *A Woman Speaks.* Harmondsworth: Penguin.

Piaget, J. (1977) *The Origin of Intelligence in the Child.* Harmondsworth: Penguin.

Pirsig, R. (1991) *Lila.* London: Corgi.

Radhakrishnan (1932) *An Idealist View of Life.* London: Allen & Unwin.

Richardson, M. (1991) *Poetry as Prayer.* Unpublished.

Rogers, C. (1987) Interview by M. Baldwin, in M. Baldwin and V. Satir (eds) *The Use of Self in Therapy.* London and New York: Haworth Press.

Rycroft, C. (1968) *Imagination and Reality.* London: The Hogarth Press.

Solomon, M. (1988) *Beethoven Essays.* Cambridge, Mass.: Harvard University Press.

Spengler, O. (1962) *The Decline of the West.* London: Allen & Unwin.

Steiner, G. (1989) *Real Presences.* London: Faber & Faber.

Stern, D.N. (1985) *The Interpersonal World of the Infant.* New York: Basic Books.

Stevens, A. (1983) *Archetype: A Natural History of the Self.* New York: Quill.

Stevens, W. (1957) *The Necessary Angel: Essays on Reality and the Imagination.* New York: Vintage Books.

Tillich, P. (1956) *The New Being.* London: SCM Press.

Wertheim, E.S. (1975) 'Person environment interaction: the significance of autonomy and competence', *British Journal of Medical Psychology* 48(1): 1–8.

Wilde, O. (1930) *The Picture of Dorian Gray*, in *Plays, Prose Writings and Poems.* London: Dent.

Wilde, O. (1954) 'The soul of man under socialism', in *Selected Essays and Poems.* Harmondsworth: Penguin.

Winnicott, D.W. (1965) *The Maturational Processes and the Facilitating Environment.* London: The Hogarth Press.

Wolf, E.S. (1988) *Treating the Self.* New York and London: Guilford Press.

Wordsworth, J. (1969) *The Music of Humanity.* New York: Harper & Row.

Zweig, S. (1939) *Beware of Pity.* London: Cape.

Zweig, S. (1943) *The World of Yesteryear.* London: Cassell.

Index

Ackroyd, P. 34
affect attunement 9, 20, 22, 23–5, 58–9, 60, 73
affect tracking 60
affective reaction: secondary effects 51; three types 49–50
agency 18, 30, 59, 66, 73, 82; importance of 62; as initiator of therapy 61; as power 61; as vital function of self 62
alienation 13, 21
alter ego 6, 35, 63
ambition, pole of 30
Anderson, S. and Hopkins, P. 111–12
anticipatory function of art 2
archaic need 7, 29, 36, 48, 67–8
archaic selfobject transference 65
archetypes 4–5, 10
attachment behaviour 29
attunement 23–5, 86
Auden, W.H. 32
authentic being 69, 109, 112, 113
authentic relating 92
autonomy 73–4

Beethoven, L. van 103
behaviour 29, 113; allowable 46–7
behavioural responsivity 23
bi-polar self 5–7, 30–5, 56; examples of 7–8
borderline disorders 56
Buber, M. 9–11, 71, 75, 79, 82, 85, 92, 107

Campbell, J. 11
collective unconscious 4
communication 19, 75
compensatory structures 44
consciousness, significance of 16
core relatedness 19, 21
core self 4, 21; emergence of 15–19; importance of 24–5

Day Lewis, C. 69, 81
death 97–101; fear of 101; life out of 98–105
defensive structures 44–5
depressive reaction 49–50
dialogical encounter 71, 79–80, 82, 83
diary, as expression of self 111
disillusion 84
dreams 44, 71
drive psychology 3

ego states 75
Ellman, R. 32
emergent self 17, 28, 96, 110
empathic: awareness 60, 70–3, 82; failure 24, 36–7, 44, 63, 66; psychotherapy 3; resonance 9, 10, 25, 59, 61, 66, 72–3
empathy 59–60, 70–1, 73, 85; importance of 9–11; as initiator and goal 60–1; occurrence of 60
essential self, and failure 52–3
exhibitionism 28, 31, 44, 45
experience see selfobject experience

'experience-distant' approach 3
'experience-near' approach 3–4

failure *see* selfobject failure
false-self 22, 26–8, 53, 64
fantasy 71, 83, 84, 85, 86
fear 67, 72
Frame, J. 12–13, 51–2, 93–105
Freud, S. 83, 85, 111
functional self, and failure 53–5

God 115
grief/grieving 57, 96, 100, 102–3, 104, 114

halucinatory wish-fulfilment 83, 84
Herman, J.L. 65
Holroyd, M. 8, 33, 34

I-am-I 4, 9–10
I–It 9–11
I–Thou 9–10, 80
idealizing 5–6, 8, 31, 33–4, 40, 41, 44–5, 63; as relationship-independent 34; transference 3
illusion 84
individuality, achievement of 28
individuation 4, 109
infants: and illusion of omnipotence 28–9; research and observation 15–17, 25
initiative and control 73–4; macrosphere 75–6, 77; microsphere 74–5
inner world 6–7, 28, 29, 30, 67–8, 86, 95–6, 109; cultivation of 97–8; depth 100
interaction patterns: *alter-ego hungry* 55; *contact-shunning* type 55; *ideal-hungry* 55; *merger-hungry* 55; *mirror-hungry* 55
internal discourse 13, 84
intersubjective relatedness 19–20, 21, 22, 23, 25
islands of consistency 18, 113

Jung, C.G. 4, 6, 10

Kepler, J. 5, 10, 82

knowing 17
Kohut, H. 1–7, 9–10, 25, 34, 36–7, 44–5, 50–1, 59, 85, 92

Laing, R.D. 107, 110–11
Lawrence, D.H. 3–4, 37–44, 50, 53, 70, 114
Lee, G. 33–4
life crises 48
life–death polarity 99–105
light–dark polarity 99
Lorenz, K. 10
love 114

Macleod, S. 114
Meares, R. 79, 113
Merton, T. 109
Milton, John 98
mirror transference 3
mirroring 5–6, 8, 23, 25, 30, 31, 40, 42, 44, 49, 51, 62, 63, 72, 86, 98; as relationship-bound 34
misattunement 22–3
mother–child relationship 10
mutuality 77, 78

narcissism 28, 46–7; two sides of 8
narcissistic: disorders 56; hurt 54; rage 50–1
Nin, A. 110–11

other 18, 28, 83, 107

participation 76–7
personal sincerity 69
Piaget, J. 82
Pirsig, R. 109
playspace 79
pleasure principle 83
poetry, and prayer 111–12
power 73, 74
psychic energy 46
psychic intimacy 20

Radhakrishnan 81, 82
reality 95; awareness of 85–6; clear perception of 81–2; defined 83–4; of object 84–5
reality principle 83

reciprocity 5, 9, 10–11, 73, 74, 82, 85, 92, 106, 113
regression 48
relationship bridge 78–9
responsibility 61–2
Rilke, R.M. 98, 114
Rogers, C. 108, 115
Rycroft, C. 83–6, 87, 92

selective attunement 23
self: awakening of 59; building of 37–44; and changing social structures 108–9; clinical relevance of 1, 2, 10, 13–14; developmental stages 15–22; disorder in 48–57; duality of 31; effects on 1–2; essential nature of 26–8; establishment and consolidation of 96; and experience 28–30; fragmented 54–5; as going out 96; grounding of 39; over-burdened 55; over-stimulated 54; recovery in 58–68; search for 37–44; as two-stage process 106–7; under-stimulated 54; weakened areas of 3, 67
self-affectivity 18
self-affirmation 72
self-agency 18, 59, 61
self-awareness 76
self-boundary 35, 54, 76
self-coherence 18
self-cohesion 49, 54
self-confidence 66
self-consummation 70
self-definition 16, 76
self-determination 111
self-development 110
self-disclosure 114
self-discovery 69–70, 71–2
self-esteem 46–7, 49; and failure 56–7
self-expression 51
self-function 23–5; understanding of 15
self-history 18
self-knowledge 95, 110
self-realization 8, 37, 38–44, 108

self-regulation 36–7
selfhood 26, 28
selfobject 6–7; concept of 12; deficiency 49; metaphorical definition 19; non-personal world of 39
selfobject experience 7, 17–19, 36, 86, 96, 106; adversarial 35; deficiencies in 36; developing 87–92; immediate function 28–30; structural function 30–5; true–false function 26–8; as vivifying virtue 87
selfobject failure: and affective reaction 49–52; direct effects of 52–7
separation 76–7
Shaw, G.B. 7–8, 45, 46, 110; as 'doing' person 31, 33–4
Solomon, M. 103
spirit/spirituality 11–12, 28, 79, 93, 106; in action 93–105; in essence 81–92
Steiner, G. 13, 115
Stern, D.N. 8–9, 15–17, 20, 22–4, 55–6, 60, 84, 112
Stevens, A. 4, 5
structural self 30–5; and failure 56–7
subjective–objective dichotomy 21

Tennyson, A. 104
tension arc 34–5
therapeutic metaphor 24
therapeutic relationship 20, 29, 63–6, 107; and control 74–5; and differentiation 78; and empathic awareness 70–3; participation and separation 76–8, 79; and patient dependence 3; and power reciprocity 73–4, 77; primary goals 69
therapist: as idealized selfobject 67; task of 63, 63–4, 73
therapy 70; and awakening of self 59–68; as dialogical encounter 68; termination of 71, 76, 77–9
Tillich, P. 11
transference 7, 44, 64–5, 77, 79–80, 92; selfobject 73; two types of 113

transitional objects 29
transmuting internalization 37, 43
traumatic transference reaction 64–5
true-self 26–8, 71
twinship experience *see* alter ego

values and ideals, pole of 30
verbal self 20–2

Wertheim, E.S. 73

whole-person relatedness 82
wholeness 81
Wilde, O. 7–8, 45; as 'being' person
    31–4
Winnicott, D.W. 29, 84, 85
Wolf, E.S. 31
Wordsworth, J. 90–1
Wordsworth, W. 86–92, 104

Zweig, S. 1, 13, 58–9, 63